The IMAM'S Daughter

The
IMAM'S
Daughter

My Desperate Flight to Freedom

Hannah Shah

ZONDERVAN®

ZONDERVAN.com/
AUTHORTRACKER
follow your favorite authors

ZONDERVAN

The Imam's Daughter
Copyright © 2010 by Hannah Shah

This title is also available as a Zondervan ebook.
Visit www.zondervan.com/ebooks.

This title is also available in a Zondervan audio edition.
Visit www.zondervan.fm.

Requests for information should be addressed to:

Zondervan, *Grand Rapids, Michigan* 49530

Library of Congress Cataloging-in-Publication Data

Shah, Hannah.
        The Imam's daughter / Hannah Shah.
            p.   cm.
        Includes bibliographical references.
        ISBN 978-0-310-32575-8 (hardcover)
            1. Shah, Hannah. 2. Christian converts from Islam — Great Britain — Biography.
        I. Title.
        BV2626.4.S52A3   2010
        248.2'46092 — dc22   2009053156
                                                                                              [B]

Cover design: Curt Diepenhorst
Cover photography: Irene Lamprakou / DAJ / Getty Images®
Interior design: Beth Shagene

Printed in the United States of America

10 11 12 13 14 15 /DCI/ 23 22 21 20 19 18 17 16 15 14 13 12 11 10 9 8 7 6 5 4 3 2 1

To My Little Chicken —

You are precious and I love you.
I pray that your life will be built on love (Ephesians 4:17).
H.S.

&

For Mum.
D.L.

Author's Note

This is a true story — though some identifying details have been changed for reasons of safety — and is in no way a denigration of Islam in general. It is a personal account of my own life experiences, and deals with the way that Islam was practiced within my own community, as I witnessed it growing up.

www.hannahshah.com

Contents

The
IMAM'S
Daughter

The ultimate weakness of violence is that it is a descending spiral, begetting the very thing it seeks to destroy. Instead of diminishing evil, it multiplies it. Through violence you may murder the liar, but you cannot murder the lie ... Through violence you may murder the hater, but you do not murder hate ... So it goes. Returning violence for violence multiplies violence, adding deeper darkness to a night already devoid of stars. Darkness cannot drive out darkness: only light can do that. Hate cannot drive out hate: only love can.

DR. MARTIN LUTHER KING JR.

And now, these three continue forever:
Faith, hope and love,
And the greatest of these is love.

1 CORINTHIANS 13:13 NCV

CHAPTER 1

My Street

❀

From my childhood — the images sketchy and opaque, a splash of color here and there among darkness — I remember one thing clearly: my street. East Street, in Bermford, the north of England. Two rows of identical, brick-built Victorian houses and a shady park at the north end like leafy branches atop a blood-red trunk. I saw the gnarled trees as fanged monsters among whose knotted, bestial shadows our childhood games darted.

I flitted — daydreaming, pigtailed, hand-me-down mary janes rubbing the long spine of the cracked sidewalk — from house to house. Doors were always left open, and there was no fear of being robbed. I could wander down to my friend Amina's place whenever I felt like it. I was welcome to stay for as long as I wanted. If I was out for more than three or four hours, someone would come looking for me — my mother or one of my brothers. But it was still a kind of freedom for a little child.

I'd be offered a drink of Pakistani tea — water boiled

with tea leaves, hot milk, heaps of sugar, and sometimes cardamom—and something to eat. It was chocolate digestives or Rich Tea biscuits one day and curry or *chapattis* the next. Hours later I found my way home, skipping past window after window blooming yellow into the dark soil of night.

It was the 1980s. We were Pakistani. We were British. We were East Street.

My mother made *chapattis* with wholemeal flour. She kneaded it with water to form dough, then took a fist-sized blob, rolled it out into a flat circle on a *chapatti* iron, and cooked it until dark spots appeared on its surface. She made *parathas*, rolling out the dough into pancakes and placing them on a long-handled *tava* pan. As she tossed them in the oil, each one puffed up like a doughy balloon.

We ate with our hands, using the *chapatti* or *paratha* to scoop. Mum made *samosas* with spiced minced meat, or potato and peas. She made *pakoras* out of slices of onion and fresh chili peppers, coated in a gram flour batter and dropped into sizzling-hot oil. I watched them cook below the surface, watching for them to rise, golden brown, like fried chicken nuggets.

Across the street lived an Armenian family, a mother and her one son—one of the few families on our street who weren't of Pakistani Muslim origin. The Armenian mother tried to communicate with Mum, but her English was very limited. Mum told us to call her "Auntie" as a traditional sign of respect, but Dad didn't agree.

He refused to show respect to anyone except other Pakistani Muslims—not even the Indian Muslims who lived around the corner on Jenna Street.

Armenian "Auntie" brought us Armenian food and Mum took Pakistani delicacies to them. Mostly, we were given vegetarian hotpots—aubergines, potatoes, and carrots stewed in a salty, peppery sauce. Before we were allowed to eat, Mum went through the food with a fork, checking for any suspect meat. If there wasn't any, we were free to tuck in.

When the weather was good, Armenian Auntie dragged a pinewood chair into her front yard. She sat there with her son, soaking up the sun and peeling potatoes. We talked in passing, across the green picket fence, but we never went inside. She understood she wasn't welcome in our home, and she didn't invite us into her house, either. Thankfully, she couldn't have known the lack of welcome was because my father hated white people.

A few doors down lived a second Armenian family —mother, father, and daughter. They went to mass at an Orthodox Christian church and growled at everyone else on the street. Several other houses were filled with a rotating cast of renters—black students from the Congo, Cameroon, and Algeria.

Everyone else on our street was a Pakistani Muslim. The adults dressed as they would have in a village in Pakistan: women and men wore *shalwar kamiz*, a loose, matching smock top and trousers. The women's were more colorful, while the men had baggy trousers, in more sober, masculine colors, like browns, grays, and whites. Dad was always dressed in a white *shalwar kamiz* with a *topi*, a traditional Punjabi skullcap, on his head.

Most of the men changed when they went to work. They seemed to shrug on a Western skin when they left our street and entered the city as taxi drivers, policemen, engineers, and salespeople. None of the women of my parents' generation worked, but some of the younger ones took jobs as secretaries or helpers in shops, at least until they married. They always kept themselves properly covered and showed appropriate modesty.

Four doors down lived my Great-Uncle Kramat and Great-Auntie Sakina. They were our surrogate grandparents, for our real ones were back in the village in Pakistan. I didn't entirely like going to their house. I was scared of Uncle Kramat, who could be quite fierce with his long, white beard and bushy eyebrows joining together in the middle. He and Auntie Sakina gossiped about my parents while they drank tea and watched television.

Uncle Kramat and Auntie Sakina had three grown children—two married sons, Ahmed and Saghir, and a married daughter, Kumar, all of whom lived with Uncle Kramat and Auntie Sakina. That wasn't unusual on our street.

None of Uncle Kramat and Auntie Sakina's children had any children. The neighbors gossiped darkly that this was a punishment from Allah. Uncle Kramat was not a very religious man — not in the way it was defined on our street. He didn't always go to the mosque. And he smoked *all* the time, despite knowing that the Qur'an says: "Do not kill yourselves."[1]

Good luck or bad luck was often attributed to someone's moral or spiritual behavior. Uncle Kramat's lack of piety was understood as the reason for his children's infertility; yet the gossipers ignored the fact that Ahmed, Saghir, and Kumar had married their first cousins. In any case, it was agreed the entire family ought to accept Allah's will and stop such nonsense as in-vitro fertilization.

Islam is first and foremost submission to Allah's will. Indeed, a believer is often spoken of as "the slave of God."[2] There is a common misconception that the primary meaning of Islam is peace, but that is true only in that a believer finds peace by submitting to Allah's will.

❊ ❊ ❊

My best friend was Amina. She had unruly dark hair that fell to her shoulders in a wild tangle. Neither of us thought it was very pretty, but she had to live with it. Amina's sister, Ruhama, with her thick, wavy hair, was considered by far the prettier of the two. Both girls were paler-skinned than my sisters and me.

"She's so pretty!" people in the street and at school would remark of Ruhama. "She's got such lovely hair, and such pale skin!" When I heard this, I presumed that dark skin was less beautiful.

Amina's household seemed more relaxed than mine. Her parents didn't pray regularly, and apart from her Qur'an lessons Amina was rarely made to read the holy book. Neither she nor Ruhama ever had to wear a *hijab*, our Muslim headscarf, when they were outside the house.

My father was the community *imam*, our religious teacher and leader; so I wore a *hijab* at all times.

Amina, Ruhama, and I played hopscotch constantly. The paving stones were laid in offset squares, so we simply wrote numbers inside each. If our feet touched the cracks in the pavement, we were out. We started timing each other — counting from one to one hundred — and seeing who could do it the fastest. My attention often wandered mid-hop, and I never beat Amina and Ruhama.

My world wasn't always happy, and my only escape was to make another one.

I spent much of my free time alone in my room, reading. I made up stories and drew, over and over, a small cottage with a pretty flower garden. My real home had a tiny backyard where Mum grew mint and coriander; she had no time or space for flowers.

✸ ✸ ✸

On the fifth of November, Bonfire Night transformed our street. In the days leading up to the festivities, everyone joined forces to build a massive tower of waste wood, fallen branches, and old packing crates. Each household bought whatever fireworks and sparklers it could afford.

18

November was cold, so we wrapped ourselves in woolen scarves and hats as we waited for the fire to be lit. I loved that moment—the wonderful, tingling anticipation of our woodpile flaring in a breathy whoosh of fire.

The men doused the wood in old sump oil and warned us to stand back. Suddenly—in a throaty *whump* —burning heat and sparks were thrown across our faces and high into the dark sky. We roasted potatoes and marshmallows over the flames, warmed our hands and faces, and munched bonfire toffee.

It was the one time of year when everyone on our street was united—Pakistani Muslims, Christians, Armenians, African students—everyone except my father. He stood outside our house, watching the flames with crossed arms and a scowl that cast flickering shadows across his fore-head. Dad hated seeing people have fun.

Because Christmas and Easter were Christian affairs, our community wasn't allowed to celebrate them. But Dad didn't understand Bonfire Night, because all he knew about his adopted country was that it was a land of immorality, populated by infidels. In his eyes, Bonfire Night was a white English affair, but he couldn't think of any religious justification for banning it. Everyone enjoyed it so much he would have had a real fight on his hands if he had tried to stop the festivities. Instead, he never joined in and made sure everyone saw his disapproval.

❋ ❋ ❋

Near the end of our street lived the last white British lady in the neighborhood. She owned a black Jack Russell that we called, predictably, Jack. When he spotted us, he raced out of the house, growling and yapping as he ran. One day, as my friend Saira pounded down the sidewalk, Jack caught her and sank his teeth into her leg.

As soon as we heard what had happened, Mum and I went round to visit. Gingerly, Saira took the bandage off to show us the damage. There were puncture marks where Jack's teeth had gone in, and stitches all around the wound. I was impressed. Saira was given a tetanus jab in her bottom, in case Jack had poisoned her.

Saira's parents were angry. There was a Pakistani Muslim policeman who lived on a neighboring street. Anyone with a serious problem in our community always took it to him, and he told Jack's owner that the dog would have to be muzzled. But Jack never was.

Opposite Jack's place was a run-down house that crouched among thick bushes. It looked dark and mysterious, and my brothers used to say that the Bogeyman lived there. I hated walking past. I knew the Bogeyman was a monster with some horrible disfigurement on his face — why else did he stay inside all the time? I imagined he was a white person, because someone had once said: *I saw the Bogeyman; he's white like a ghost.* We told each other fearful stories of what the Bogeyman would do if he caught us. Zakir, the oldest of my brothers, said that the Bogeyman ate children for breakfast.

With the park and its monster trees — and Jack, and

the Bogeyman — the north end of our street was terrifying. As soon as I approached it, I started running, and I wouldn't stop until I reached the safe end.

But I never really got there, because I lived with the Bogeyman.

CHAPTER 2

To Pakistan, With Love

❈

My parents left a rural, agrarian life in Pakistan; in Britain Mum and Dad were blocked in by brick walls and tarmac. Months would pass in which their lives were confined almost entirely to the interior of the house, our street, and the nearby mosque. My mother relied on the nearby shops that sold *halal* meat, spices, okra, and *chapatti* flour. East Street was a Pakistani village in brick and mortar, shrunk down to a single British block. Mum never left the street and rarely left the house. Her responsibilities overruled her love of the outdoors.

Mum and Dad ran from the poverty trap of rural Pakistan.

An English town had running water, electricity, free education, and shops crammed full of every good imaginable. They had none of this in the Pakistani villages. There, toilets were nothing more than holes in the ground and schooling was basically non-existent. My father's education had stopped at age eleven. From then on he went to the *madrassa*, a religious school that solely teaches the Qur'an. My mother attended her village school for less than one year, after which she was barely able to read or write. We spoke to our parents in Punjabi or, occasionally, Urdu—but never English.

My father was in his late twenties when he immigrated to the United Kingdom. He had been a farmer in the Punjab, an area on the border between India and Pakistan. He was a Deobandi Sunni Muslim, a strand of Islam popular across many of the tribal areas of northern India, Pakistan, and Afghanistan. Dad first lived in a rented house in Lancashire with more than a dozen other Pakistani men from the same tribal area. None of them spoke English, but they had little need of it, either at home or at work.

The men came to work in the textile factories. As soon as they could, they helped each other buy houses. They hardly ever spent money on anything besides food and housing. Dad and another man saved up their earnings for several years and bought a house together in my hometown—bought it outright with no mortgage. Two years later their wives came to join them.

Mum and Dad were married before he left for England. It was an arranged marriage in accordance with tradition. Mum came from an impoverished rural area, so she jumped at the opportunity to move abroad and to better her life. Later, as more and more Pakistani immigrants clustered together on East Street, the white English people moved out.

My father disliked non-Muslims. This was the sixties and seventies—a time of flower power, of drugs and free love, of men wearing "weird clothes" and growing their hair long. My parents didn't approve of any of this, and they didn't like the disrespectful way English children spoke to their parents. Neither did they appreciate the lack of English community spirit, and so they created their own Pakistani Muslim community. Even as they looked to England for economic opportunity, they were determined English culture would not pollute their expatriate community.

At home, Dad was distant. He spent his time cloistered with his holy book, continually murmuring verses while fingering his *tasbih*, Muslim prayer beads which look nearly identical to Catholic rosary beads. Some are made of wood, some of marble, and the ninety-nine beads are arranged with four exactly the same followed by one slightly larger. Over long, solitary hours, my father worked the tips of his fingers from bead to bead.

Dad held his *tasbih* at all times, even walking down the street. He had little *tasbihs* sent from Pakistan for my brothers and me. By the time I was four, he'd taught me to flick the beads through my fingers while reciting the ninety-nine names of Allah—*Irahma*, the Merciful; *Rahim*, the Forgiving; *Malik*, the Sovereign—my thin lips and thinner fingers focused on the work of holiness.

To my East Street mind, these were foreign words,

syllables I could say but not understand. My faithfulness was ordered by my father. I learned these mysterious words to please him. The day I spoke all ninety-nine by heart, Dad's face remained impassive; he pulled me out in front of his guests and made me perform the *tasbih*.

The more he withheld any appreciation, the more I felt a desperate hunger to earn his blessing.

Dad's life, like that of many men on our street, was defined by religious duties. His main concerns were praying five times a day and going to the mosque to preach. Often he traveled to Lancaster, Manchester, or Birmingham for religious events at other mosques. He had no hobbies outside his religious life, except for watching television—preferably a video of a holy man giving a lesson or some *qawwali* music, a style of Sunni singing popular in Pakistan. His social life was limited to talking with his male friends, usually in the men's lounge in our house. Life, for him, was simple, serious, and necessarily hostile to outside intrusion.

Dad was not handy. If a light fitting was loose, my dad would order my brothers to fix it, or he would ring up Uncle Ahmed. Such worldly repairs were beneath him. There was far more honor in being the *Imam* than being a bus driver or a handyman—so Dad did more to honor Ahmed by being his *Imam* than Ahmed did to Dad by doing odd jobs around the home.

When I was three years old, my parents took me to visit Pakistan. We traveled to my father's home village of Pindi Khan, a tiny, mud-walled village in the Punjab, sandwiched between the North-West Frontier Province and Kashmir.

It was the rainy season. I remember the village being surrounded by green fields split by a rushing, clear blue river. Everyone in Pindi Khan is related—cousins, second cousins, second cousins twice removed—because people only marry within their clan lines. Intermarriage is part of the defense system of clans who seem to be permanently at war.

Life in Pindi Khan is simple. People earn a little money selling wheat, milk, cattle, goats, and eggs. Animals are used to plow, reap, and sow. The local boys are educated either at the *madrassa* or the village school, while few girls are educated. The *madrassa* is better funded than the public school and seen as providing a better education.

We traveled on a *tonga*, a traditional horse and cart. Dad kept a house in the village, brick-built, with several rooms arranged around a central courtyard. Each room was flat-roofed to allow for sitting and sleeping in the open air.

Shortly after our arrival, my parents were drinking morning tea in the courtyard. The gate was open, and I wandered out. When Mum went to look for me, she found me in the middle of a field, sitting beneath an enormous cow. The cow seemed to be standing guard over me, as if I was her calf. Mum and one of Dad's sisters burst out laughing even as they rushed over and whisked me away from the danger of being trampled.

Later we were sitting in the field among the goats. I was playing with some coins, and when a goat nuzzled up to me I offered it one. The goat licked the coin — a *paisa*, worth less than a penny — straight out of my hand and swallowed it. Mum had to tell everyone in the village, her laughter growing with each retelling.

By the end of our time there my mum had showed me off to the whole village and had told many stories of life in another country, a country which seemed like a dream world to the villagers.

Back in the UK, Mum was proud she had taken her eldest daughter home to Pakistan. She was forever telling visitors about it: "Hannan went to the village, you know. She was adopted by a cow and even fed a *paisa* to a goat! She seemed so at home there in Pakistan, a good Muslim country."

Had I? It was a repeated line throughout my childhood — *Hannan seemed so at home there* — but I couldn't remember exactly. My memories of the village were a hazy composite of my three-year-old recall and my mother's stories of what her childhood had been like.

Mum was forever reminiscing. She painted life in the village with expansive colors: neighbors sharing houses, friends helping friends gather crops in the fields, women cooking curry and *chapattis* with measures of flour and laughter. Mum loved telling the story of how she left her village and came to England, and her words were always driven by a wistful wind. Every East Streeter seemed to share the romantic conviction that villagers were one big happy family.

Yet letters from aunts, uncles, and cousins in Pakistan were passed around, letters that gave us a more realistic sense of Pakistani life and culture. We read about uncles who traveled to places like Dubai or Saudi Arabia to work when there were no jobs in the village. We heard news of births, marriages, and deaths in our extended family; but most of this meant as little to me as reading about strangers on the front page of the newspaper display I passed every day at the corner of East and Jenna Street.

My parents wanted us to understand Pakistan. We were told to read books in Urdu about the post-colonial partition of India that created Pakistan. We were supposed to learn about the life of Mohammed Ali Jinnah, the man who oversaw partition and became the first governor-general of Pakistan. But I lived in England, and it was England that felt like home.

Whenever we received family news from Pakistan, my brothers would mutter: "God! We're so glad we don't live there!" They were careful to do so in English, so my parents couldn't understand. Britain was, for my brothers, a land of opportunity when compared to rural Pakistan. Luxuries like running water, electricity, and paved roads were nice, but more than that, my brothers understood the restrictions they would live under in Pakistan.

No more watching soccer on television, hanging out with their schoolmates, wearing Western clothes, or listening to pop bands. In Pakistan they would spend their time at *madrassa* memorizing the Qur'an, praying at the mosque, and working on the farm. Plenty of cousins in Pakistan led exactly that life, and none of us envied them.

There were people on our street who seemed to pine for that sort of existence. We called them *Pakis*. The word signified someone who was wedded to the old ways. My sister Sabina proved to be a *Paki* herself. After Mum and Dad took her back to the village, she never stopped talking about it. "Oh, I loved it there," Sabina told us. "Everyone is so religious."

Pakistan has this, Pakistan has that. Listening to her got old, fast. Sometimes we'd call her a *Paki* to her face, a label she seemed almost proud of. Of course, if an outsider had called any of us a *Paki*, there would have been trouble. *Paki* was also a racist taunt that each of us would have thrown our way at one time or another.

Gora was our term for a white person and, like the term *Paki*, it could mean several things. When I mentioned the *goray* at the end of our street to my sister, I was simply being descriptive—*gora* meant "white person." In my father's mouth, however, *gora* became a racist epithet. He didn't hide his abhorrence of white people and their ways from us, but in public he seemed to be happy mixing with people from all different backgrounds.

A contradictory view of the West permeated rural Pakistani society. On one hand, everything Western was hateful; on the other, it was a sign of real achievement to have family living and working in the West. "Ali has done well," so-and-so would remark. "His son has been to the UK, and he got a job and married there."

Whatever job someone had secured overseas — even if it was delivering pizzas — he would still be able to earn enough to return to Pakistan a wealthy man. When Mum and Dad went back to their village, they were treated like celebrities. Emigration is one of the few routes out of the grinding poverty of rural life that otherwise continues unchanged from generation to generation.

My parents initially viewed Britain as a temporary sojourn. The plan was to earn money and return home. Yet they, like many other immigrants, decided to settle down. At the same time, they resented British culture and tried to isolate themselves from it.

It didn't take my father long to realize the British education system was vastly superior to anything available in rural Pakistan. He knew it would give his sons a much better chance of material success. He didn't care about his daughters' education — they were only good for marrying off and having children — but he wanted his sons to prosper.

I was the fourth child and the first girl. At first, my brothers were happy to have a little sister. Zakir was my eldest brother, Mum's favorite, and a know-it-all. He stuck up for me in school or on the street if he saw anyone being nasty to me. But in the privacy of our home, my father and brothers were nasty to me, for I was "only a girl."

My next brother was Raz, and he was the most religious of the boys. He wasn't radical, just spiritual. From an early age, the mosque was his life. He didn't do well at school, and he wasn't bothered about studying mainstream subjects.

My third—and favorite—brother was Billy. Billy means "cat" in Punjabi, a nickname he earned with his slinky grace and rakish good looks. He was charming and considerate. When Billy tried to help in the house, my father stopped him. That wasn't the right sort of work for boys. Billy was the only one who was ever vaguely nice to me. Billy was also the family peacemaker. We were forever fighting over what to watch on television, but Billy would try to talk everyone into taking turns.

After me came two more girls. The first was Sabina. Like Raz, she was very religious, though her faith was far more conservative. Sabina grew up with an active dislike of English culture. She didn't like going to school or mixing with boys. She had almost no white friends. With her natural affinity for traditional Pakistani culture, she was the perfect daughter for Mum and Dad that I could never be.

Several years later Aliya was born. Pretty and dainty, she was Dad's favorite girl. He was quite soft with her. She would sit on his lap and fire questions at him: *If you pray like this, what will happen?* To my amazement, he would answer her.

In our culture, girls are less welcome. We are in need of constant protection—and not for our own good but for the family's honor. If a daughter goes off the rails, it brings more shame on her family than if a son does. In Pakistani culture, gossip is always about girls.

The culture on our street was very much centered around how you could gain honor, how you could maintain that honor, or how you could avoid bringing shame on yourself or the family. The women were obsessed with shame and honor, because they knew that in Pakistani culture the honor of the community was carried by each woman in that community. On our street, the gossip taught us what was appropriate behavior and what was not. It taught us to fear shame and seek honor.

By the time I was born Dad had left his factory job and started working as the local *Imam*. He didn't earn a wage. Instead, he survived on benefits and on what the community donated.

We didn't have many luxuries. Most of our clothes came from charity shops, and we females shared one room together. Like many Pakistani couples, my parents never slept in the same room. Dad slept in the front lounge. Zakir had his own room, while Raz and Billy shared.

My sisters and I wore traditional *shalwar kamiz* without fail. These were made by Mum on a Singer electric sewing machine. She sewed clothes in the kitchen when we were at school. Other women on the street paid her a little to make outfits for weddings or festivals. If money was tight, Mum put the money she earned toward the family food budget; if it wasn't, she might buy us a treat. One thing she never did was spend it on herself.

❋ ❋ ❋

From the day I was born I was steeped in Islam. It dominated our lives from dawn to dusk. My father taught me the Five Pillars of Islam, the foundations of our faith. Anyone who adhered to the Five Pillars—the declaration of faith; giving money to the poor; fasting during the holy month of Ramadan; *Hajj*, the pilgrimage to Mecca; and praying five times a day—was on the path to Paradise, he said.

From the age of three my task was to learn the Qur'an and bring honor to our family. The Qur'an must be learned and spoken in classic Arabic, the original language in which it was written. My parents' native tongues are Urdu and Punjabi, and we usually spoke Punjabi at home. My dad ran formal Qur'an lessons for all the children on our street below the age of five. Every weekday we crowded into the guest room at the front of the house—and woe to any of us who got my father's lessons wrong.

On one wall of the lounge was a picture of the *Kaaba*, the holiest place of Islam. The *Kaaba* is a cube-like building in Mecca, Saudi Arabia. It stands about fifteen meters high, ten or twelve wide, and is draped in the *kiswah*, a black silk cloth embroidered with Qur'anic verses. It is said to have been built by Abraham and Ishmael. Dad taught us that the *Kaaba* is venerated because it contains the first Qur'an upon which the Prophet Mohammed recorded the holy word of God. (In fact, the *Kaaba* is empty, apart from a meteorite called the Black Stone embedded in the southeast corner. As a child, the holes in my father's knowledge and faith were as invisible to me as they were to him.)

On the opposite wall, framed gold lettering proclaimed in Arabic: "Mohammed, peace be upon him." Below that was a cabinet containing crockery only used on special occasions, and two glass snow globes. One was a snowstorm over the *Kaaba*, the other a storm of snowflakes swirling around the name of the Prophet Mohammed. We never got them out and played with them. To have done so would have been disrespectful. It would have attracted my father's wrath, and that, I knew, was best avoided.

On the top shelf of the cabinet rested a number of Qur'ans. It is respectful to keep the holy book in a high place. Each was covered in a tiny cloth sleeve made by Mum from odd bits of sewing material. During Qur'an lessons, we sat in a square of twelve, facing inward, with Dad at the head. Each of us had a wooden *rail*—a bookstand—with an Arabic dictionary, or a Surah (chapter) of the Qur'an, propped on it. Boys and girls sat together, without uniforms, but these classes were joyless. One by one, we'd sit by Dad and recite the day's lesson.

My father was strict. No one ever misbehaved. Even a whisper to a friend would earn a sharp whack. The broom handle Dad kept in one corner ensured our compliance.

If we didn't recite the Arabic perfectly, we were beaten. We understood the words had a particular spiritual significance in Arabic that was lost if spoken in any other language, such as the English we all understood.

We were never taught the actual meaning of the words we recited—just the pitch-perfect Arabic pronunciation. As we said the same sentences over and over, sometimes for an hour or more, I recognized proper names, like "Allah" and "Mohammed." Beyond that, I didn't have a clue what any of it meant. None of us questioned anything or asked for explanations. We were too scared of my father.

I learned to read the first *Surah* (chapter) of the Qur'an pitch-perfect when I was just five years old. I was one of the first in the class to do so. Dad was forever encouraging the other girls and boys, but never me. I learned that *Surah* by heart to win his heart, but the effort was wasted. Dad was clear that he never wanted a daughter. In private, he told me I was an evil, cursed girl. He said it was up to me to prove I wasn't "unworthy of Allah."

Because my father was the *Imam*, my parents were pillars of the community. My father had an exalted status. To outsiders, he appeared sweet and gentle. He spoke almost in a whisper, smiled a lot, and played the role of a truly spiritual and peaceable person.

"What a lovely father you have," I heard time after time.

In private, my father was cruel and hateful, prone to

fits of rage and violence. He beat Mum. Even at the age of four, I didn't have to be told this was wrong. Yet, like any child, I still wanted my father to love and be proud of me.

People from the community called my father *Hajji*, meaning one who has been on the pilgrimage to Mecca. They addressed my mother by the feminine form, *Hajjin*. People saw Dad as their source of guidance and wisdom, and they would come to seek his advice. My father was always ready with a response—uncertainty or ambivalence were unheard of. Having a daughter who misbehaved would have been the ultimate dishonor for my father.

I never really stood a chance, for I was born a rebel.

CHAPTER 3

Lessons

❋

My life was an exercise in reading between the lines. Rules were rarely specified. I had to work out what was allowed and what was not, by listening to the gossip. Even having a white person visit your house could incite gossip.

We'd all heard Dad express his views on white people and their decadent culture. He was forever ranting about *goray*, the godless, heathen fornicators surrounding our street. They drank alcohol and were sexually loose. We had only to look at the clothes they wore to know the truth of this. Women freely showed off flesh — arms, legs, and even cleavage! — to tempt men. My father wanted none of his offspring to have anything to do with *goray*.

My brothers hung out with other Pakistani Muslim boys. But they did have white friends at school. Whenever Dad wasn't around they talked about friends with exotic names like Tim, Andy, and Peter. They knew better than to try to bring their *goray* friends home. Dad would refuse them entry. Once, Zakir walked back from school with his white friend, Dave, but he found an excuse to make Dave wait for him at the front gate.

The prohibition against contact with white people was entirely my father's. His fear was two-fold: he believed it was his religious duty to reject foreigners, and he worried that English ways would somehow infect his family and pull us away from the straight and narrow. Mum didn't share such fears. However, my father's will ruled our house. She knew very well that none of us were allowed to have white visitors, even as little children.

When I was four, I befriended two sisters, Jane and Susan, at nursery school. Mum and I often walked most of the way home with them, since they lived two streets past ours. Mum was forever smiling and laughing with them. When she brought me cookies or some toffee sweets, she'd make sure I shared them with Jane and Susan.

At home everything was different. It was fine for Jane and Susan to play with me in the backyard, but they had to be kept out of the house. If Dad was around, they weren't welcome even in the yard. For Mum it was a delicate balancing act. She didn't want to be unwelcoming to my friends, but she'd been taught never to question her husband or defy his will — doubly so when her husband was the community *Imam*.

Jane, nearer to me in age, was my best friend. Girls make and break friends quite a lot at that age, but we were close for a long time. She was self-confident and ebullient, not introverted like me. Jane and I sat next to each other at school. She loved the sound of her own voice, and I could listen for hours — we were a perfect match. The time I spent with Jane was my escape from a suffocating home. But not even with a best friend like her could I forget my father.

❊ ❊ ❊

Mum was serving Dad curry in the back lounge. The front room was reserved for receiving male guests, and the back lounge was where we gathered to watch television — the only activity we ever did as a family. My mother handed my father his plate of curry. I watched him scoop a handful with a piece of *chapatti*, but as he began to chew, his face turned dark as thunder.

"This isn't cooked properly," he snapped. "It's cold! You stupid woman! I can't eat this!"

He hurled the food at the wall. The plate smashed, sending brown fingers of food groping down the wallpaper. Dad leapt to his feet, yelling at Mum. As she backed away in terror, he began screaming at her for trying to escape when he was talking. She pled with him to calm down, but he stormed after her into the kitchen.

I sat alone in the lounge, my legs pulled up to my chest. I heard the dull thump of Dad's fist smashing into Mum's body. She screamed, sucked a ragged breath, and screamed again. Every landed blow pressed my knees tighter against my chest. Mum begged Dad to stop, but the merciless pounding continued. I was sure the neighbors could hear. But Dad was the *Imam*, the definition of a holy man.

At last he stormed out of the kitchen and into the front lounge. I crept to the kitchen. I wanted to comfort Mum, and I wanted her to comfort me. She was curled in a fetal position on the floor. My father was clever in that he never hit her on her face or hands as the beatings would be evident. I reached out to her, my fingers trembling

Mum pushed me away. She pushed me away, ashamed for her four-year-old daughter to see her. When she finally inched to her feet she could barely walk, but it was her job to clean the mess. She knelt and picked up the shards of broken plate, pried the congealing curry from the wallpaper. Every motion was practiced, despite her pain. Later, Dad emerged from his room as if nothing had happened.

I soon saw the pattern. Dad beat up Mum, she cleared the mess, and all of us — her, Dad, the kids, the neighbors — pretended everything was normal. My anger made me quiver. By silently accepting the beatings, Mum was trying to protect the honor of my father and the family.

It happened at least once a month. Tepid curry. Weak tea. Wrinkled clothing. Dust on the rim of a guest's cup. We were a tree with spreading branches and a rotting core.

I lived in the hope that things would get better, that Dad would become the loving father I dreamed him to be. He would stop beating Mum. He would notice me. He would praise me, just once, for my Qur'an recitals. Life would be good if I could just be good enough.

※ ※ ※

My kindergarten teachers reported that I was kind, but far too shy. The same was true at home. Whenever guests came, I would hide in my room and read. I hardly ever spoke to my brothers. And with my father, the only communication I ever had was my Qur'an lessons, or the orders he barked at me.

School was a much happier place than home, and I always tried to excel. The headmaster was named Bill Hicks, and he had wild, curly hair and a brown mustache. He taught PE, and in his spare time he refereed for several local soccer clubs.

Each morning Mr. Hicks sat at the front of the school assembly hall and told us a story in his strong, booming voice. His tales were about everything and anything: growing up in nearby Keighley, going fishing in the rivers as a lad, playing soccer with his childhood friends, hiking with his dad in the hills, or going on an expedition to the seaside.

Even though a lot of us couldn't relate directly to what Mr. Hicks was saying, his words captivated us. His childhood, and especially his relationship with his parents, was alien to us. It was as if he was telling us about a different world, but that just made it all the more magical and thrilling. Yet despite the longing his stories conjured in me, I could hardly go home and say to my parents, "Why don't we go fishing like Mr. Hicks did when he was a kid? Or visit the seaside? Why can't we do those things?"

I decided the life of carefree, family fun that Mr. Hicks described was what white people did.

Neither of my parents ever told us stories about their own childhoods. Mum used to read us *The Hare and the Tortoise* in Urdu, but that was to help us learn the language. The nearest we got to imaginary stories was when Mum told us tales about bad little girls who ran off on their own, told lies, argued with their siblings, and disobeyed their elders. These girls were always caught and punished by nameless, faceless monsters—and they deserved it, too.

I heard those morality tales before bed each night. But soon, thanks to Dad, I would be living them.

❋ ❋ ❋

There is no formal system in Islam to enable someone to become an *imam*, a holy man or spiritual leader. My father was not the most educated man in our community, but he did seem to have an encyclopedic knowledge of the Qur'an. On East Street, that was qualification enough.

Every weekday afternoon, a white minibus rattled down our street. "Time to go to the mosque!" the driver shouted in Punjabi. I dreaded that call. The mosque was cold, dark, damp, and frightening, and our Qur'an teacher was cruel. My instincts told me to hide.

The mosque was a converted municipal library. It was strictly segregated with different rooms for male and female worshipers. An arched doorway led into the men's prayer hall—a comfortable room with wall-to-wall floral carpet. Another arched doorway led to the women's room, which had only a few threadbare rugs scattered on the floor. Those without rugs sat on the cold concrete floor, and the mosque was always freezing. Our Qur'an teacher had a portable heater to warm her, but its feeble warmth never reached us.

Our community purchased this building from the council. It was owned by the community and administered by a committee of wealthy men. Donating money to the mosque brought honor to the family, and the committee's wives ensured that everyone knew who had donated how much.

Donations funded the addition of an ablution block, where worshipers washed before prayers. There must be running water for Muslims to perform ritual *wudu* before prayers. First the face and nostrils are washed, then the ears, followed by the neck and arms—the right always before the left. Next the feet are cleaned, including toes and ankles, and finally the hands.

As we washed, we said the *Bismillah*, the central prayer of Islam—"In the name of God, most gracious, most compassionate." Then we removed our shoes and knelt on the hard floor with a flat bench in front of us.

That's how we spent the entire hour of our Qur'an lessons at the mosque. The bench was for the Qur'an to sit on, as well as a book containing the Arabic alphabet. Forgetting either was reason to be beaten with a cane.

Once I needed to use the toilet. I couldn't wait.

"Yes?" Teacher snapped. "What is it, girl?"

"May I go to the toilet, please?"

Teacher was furious at my lack of self-control. "Come here, girl! You should have gone at home!"

She took her cane and whacked me across the palm, leaving a stinging red mark. I was thoroughly humiliated in front of my friends, and I burst into tears. Only then did she let me go to the bathroom. After that, several girls were so scared they wet themselves rather than ask to be excused. That made things worse. Teacher found out, and the girls were beaten for having peed themselves.

Each of us was required to learn a verse of the Qur'an in Arabic, repeating it until we had it perfect. As the *Imam*'s daughter, I never missed a single session despite my hatred of the lessons and our teacher.

One afternoon when I heard the call to the mosque, I crawled under my bed and hid. I stayed there, barely daring to breathe, my heart pounding in the dusty silence. My rebellion terrified me. Eventually, Dad stormed into the bedroom, grabbed me, and dragged me out.

"What are you doing?" he yelled at me. "*Masjid ki gari aiya*—it's time to go to the mosque! Get in the van!"

I didn't dare argue.

Another time I hid in my brother Zakir's room. Dad

found me there, too, and he was even more enraged. I took to hiding in the wardrobe. I'd hear various doors slamming, before he flung open the wardrobe door and tried to grab me. I'd try to bolt past him, running down the stairs and out to the van.

Not all parents made their children go to the mosque lessons. Amina and Ruhama often pretended they had headaches, and their parents didn't seem to mind. I was so envious. My father rode up front in the minibus, keeping close watch on who went and who didn't. If Amina and Ruhama missed more than one mosque session in a row, he would go and have words with their parents.

My father was the *Imam*; my father was the mosque. When I hid, I was defying more than the mosque — I was defying *him*. For my father, such defiance was insufferable.

Such defiance deserved punishment.

CHAPTER 4

A Child Alone

❋

Mum only spoke a little English, polite survival phrases like "Hello, how are you?" "How are your children?" and "How is your mother?" Her only opportunity to speak English was when she picked me up from school. She understood some of what the other mothers said and got by with shrugs and nods. With Jane and Susan's mother, she tried hard to make up for her lack of words with smiles.

There was almost no need for Mum to speak English. The only time she left East Street was when she took us to school and bought our weekly groceries at Morrisons. Even there, she simply filled the cart with what she wanted and checked out in silence.

But Mum *wanted* to speak more. She wanted to be able to chat more with the other mums at school, to talk to the Armenian woman across the road. Unlike my father, she had a desire to learn.

Whenever we watched soaps like *EastEnders* and *Coronation Street*, Mum tried to repeat what the actors said. She knew the characters had different accents, and she'd imitate them—doing a Cockney for *EastEnders*, and a Mancunian from *Corrie*, as we used to call it. Her specialty was doing Ricky and Bianca, from *EastEnders*. Ricky was a car mechanic. He worked for one of the Mitchell brothers, the likeable villains played by Steve McFadden and Ross Kemp. He was forever shouting for his wife:

"Bianca! Bianca!"

Mum tried to copy the way he cried "Bianca" with a nasal sound in place of the "c." It was hilarious when Mum yelled out, "Bianca! Bianca!"—hearing the mixture of rural Punjabi meets East End accent that came out of her mouth. Mum didn't mind us laughing. In fact, she liked making us laugh. Deep down there was a bit of a joker in Mum.

One day Mr. Hicks announced that a teacher was offering to do home lessons for families struggling to learn English. The teacher's name was Edith Smith. I introduced Mum to her, and Mum spontaneously agreed that Edith could visit and teach her English.

As far as I knew, Edith Smith was the first white Englishwoman to enter the Shah family home. Mum asked her to come at a time when she knew Dad would be at the mosque. He spent every afternoon there, and all day Friday, the Muslim holy day. Edith was thin as a rake, and so tall that she towered over us. She had curly brown hair, wire-rimmed glasses, and dressed in floral skirts and blouses.

That first time she came over, she smiled and ruffled my hair. "Hello, Hannan. How are you?"

I gazed up at her and smiled back shyly. "Hello."

Miss Smith brought a bag of delicious pear drops with her, and she handed them around. That first English lesson was held in the back lounge. As I watched, Mum began grinning happily as she tried to pronounce the English words.

Mum offered Edith some tea. Mum's idea of tea time included curry and *chapattis*, followed by biscuits and a fruit salad of apples, pears, and watermelon. Edith picked at the curry, trying to be polite, even as she was gradually turning a brighter and brighter shade of red. Suddenly, she grabbed a glass of water and gulped it down in one go—she'd found a chili!

Mum didn't seem to notice Miss Smith's discomfort, because the next time she came Mum served her more curry. I brought out an entire jug of water for poor Miss Smith. It became a secret game of mine to count how many mouthfuls she took before she grabbed her glass of water.

Of course, Mum didn't tell Dad. She could trust the other women on the street to stay silent about such things. Like Mum, they all had aspects of their lives that they had to keep hidden from their men, and they had an unspoken pact never to tell. It was a sort of East Street sisterhood.

With each visit, Mum and Miss Smith understood each other better and better. When the words weren't there, they used sign language and gestures. They laughed a lot, and teased each other as if they were old friends. When lesson time came, Mum bustled about happily, tidying the lounge and fetching the exercise book in which she wrote her lessons. She kept the book hidden, tucked beneath the cover of her sewing machine.

Miss Smith brought a ray of light into Mum's world.

"How are you?" Miss Smith asked.

"I am fine, thank you," Mum replied.

At first Mum's words were stilted. But with Edith's encouragement, she was soon sailing into deeper conversational waters.

"How did you sleep?"

"I slept very well."

"How many children do you have?"

"I have six children."

"Are you married?"

Mum smiled, embarrassed. What a thing to ask — of course she was married! How could she have six children and not be?

"Yes, I am married."

"Where do your children go to school?"

And so it went. After Miss Smith left, I helped Mum practice the English alphabet and numbers, and tried to engage her in basic conversation. After those visits, Mum was noticeably happier. She was very clever, yet she was never given the chance to study and learn. Mum was like a caged bird without a chance to fly.

One day Dad came home early from the mosque. As

usual, Mum and Miss Smith were in the lounge with me. We heard the front door open and shut. Mum immediately tensed up. The lounge door opened and Dad sat down on the sofa. For a moment, he failed to notice Miss Smith, but then he caught sight of this white woman in his home. Instantly, his face darkened like a thundercloud.

"Hello," said Miss Smith, trying to smile at him.

Dad scowled back at her and buried his head in his Qur'an. Miss Smith did her best to carry on with the lesson, but a dark and menacing atmosphere had seeped into the room. Mum looked terrified. She wasn't laughing and joking with Miss Smith anymore.

When the lesson ended, Mum saw Edith to the door and went straight into the kitchen. Dad jumped up and followed her, immediately shouting.

"What are you doing bringing that *gori* into the house? A dirty *gori infidel!* In *my* house! How *dare* you?"

From where I was sitting in the lounge, I heard that first, sickening thump of fist on flesh. Mum cried out in pain, but Dad was merciless. He beat her again and again.

My brothers were upstairs. They heard Mum's screams, but they didn't react. They supported Mum when they could, but they wouldn't dare challenge Dad's violent authority.

I sat in the lounge. Minutes earlier Mum had been laughing happily with Miss Smith about her awful pronunciation. Now, for that simple, innocent pleasure, she was being savagely beaten by Dad. I was five years old and too scared to do anything but sit in silence. Finally, Dad stormed into the men's lounge, shutting himself there in a silent rage.

I crept into the kitchen. Mum had collapsed onto the floor and she was sobbing hysterically. She couldn't get up, shaking as she was with shock and pain. I tried to put my tiny arms around her, but she pushed me away. She was ashamed and embarrassed she had been beaten again and didn't want her little daughter to see her in such a state.

I stood bewildered. I longed to help Mum, to comfort her and make her life happy — as it had been a few minutes earlier. But how could I stop Dad from hitting her? Even at the age of five, I understood it was only a matter of time before he beat Mum again, and again after that.

My dad was a bad man. How could he do this to Mum — my gentle, funny mother who never hurt anyone? Dad had really worked Mum over this time, and I was sure he knew exactly what he was doing. He knew where to hit Mum to hide the damage. It was planned. It was deliberate.

Later, Mum slowly climbed to her feet, supporting herself on the counters. She tried to ignore what had happened and carry on as if everything was normal. No one in the house said a word.

A few weeks later, Mum and I were serving Dad dinner in the lounge. He took one mouthful, screamed out in rage, and threw the plate against the wall. It landed with a deafening crash, and then Dad started yelling.

"But what's wrong?" Mum asked timidly. "I've reheated the curry from yesterday. You liked it then . . . ."

"It's cold!" Dad snarled. "You think I want cold curry!"

Dad was on his feet, hitting Mum in the middle of the lounge. Without thinking, I forced my way between them.

"You're not hitting Mummy!" I cried out. I held up my arms to try to stop him. "Stop it! Stop it! Leave Mummy *alone!*"

For a moment, Dad gaped at me in utter surprise.

Then the familiar anger and hate colored his vision. Placing his right foot behind him to get a lower angle, he punched me in the stomach. I doubled over in pain, but stayed in front of Mum protectively.

Mum cowered behind me, frozen in shock by my resistance. Dad tried to shove me out of the way, but from somewhere inside I summoned superhuman strength and clung onto Mum. Infuriated, Dad began punching me all over the body.

"Get out of the way!" he screamed. "I do what I like in this house! I'm your father! You do as I say! Get out of the way!"

As I clung to my mother's body, I kept repeating the same words through my tears: "You're not hitting Mummy. You're not hitting Mummy. You're not hitting . . . "

Dad wrenched me off Mum and threw me across the room. The couch broke my fall before I could tumble to the floor. Without another word, Dad stormed off into the men's lounge. Mum ran into the kitchen to hide. Someone in the family had finally stood up to the bully, my father, and Mum was terrified of what the consequences might be.

I was alone on the couch in the suddenly silent room. I stayed there, crying, for quite a while. I was scared of what I'd done. It was an instinctive reaction to face down my father and take the blows intended for Mum. I was in great physical pain and didn't feel able to move. Eventually, I fell asleep — or perhaps I passed out — overwhelmed by the shock and trauma.

I woke later to the sound of my brothers watching television. No one paid the slightest attention to me, or asked if I was all right. The household had reverted to its nothing-to-see-here mode. No one ever said anything about that first time Dad beat me, and I never mentioned it to Mum.

I had broken the unwritten rules of the household. I was only five years old — would I dare break the rules again? Perhaps the normal way of doing things was the only way to survive. But the normal way of doing things meant watching Dad beat up Mum, and that I couldn't bear.

In fact, the normal way had already changed. My instinctive act of resistance had changed it irrevocably. From then on, instead of hitting Mum when the food wasn't right, Dad hit me. If the house wasn't perfectly clean, he beat me. I became the object of his aggression.

To start with, he beat me about once a month. But, gradually, it became more frequent. Worse still, Mum never tried to intervene. She was relieved Dad wasn't hitting her. Each time he beat me, she acted as if nothing had happened.

My mother's lack of response hurt more than any punch.

Whenever he hit me, Dad abused me verbally: "You're stupid, lazy, and useless! You're an ugly, worthless daughter!"

There was no point in yelling, because everyone pretended not to hear my cries, and no one came to help. After that first beating, I never screamed again. I simply went silent whenever the blows started raining down.

It was a lonely time. I began escaping to a different world—a land of make-believe. I imagined I was calling out for the Loneliness Birds to come rescue me. Their soft white wings would lift me up, and with the barest of flaps we would rise into the air, my hands holding tightly to their downy feathers.

The Loneliness Birds were giant white doves who flew down from the heavens to save me. Perched beside me, watching me with their wise gray eyes, they cooed soft reassurances in my ear. "*Oooh coulah ...*" This was their language, but I had been given the gift of understanding. "Climb up, climb up. Let us fly you away." They bent their legs and I clambered onto their backs.

We flew to a beautiful field bathed in sunshine. It was a sea of purple flowers, and as we descended the tang of lavender rose to greet us. The Loneliness Birds set me down in the Lavender Fields. I could run in any direction, laughing and free. The white doves stayed and watched over me—the doting, loving parents I never had.

I always played alone in those fields. No humans meant no hurt.

When Dad beat me I heard the soft, insistent thump of white wings, coming to rescue me. When Dad left, my body shut down and I fell asleep, lost in dreams of a lonely paradise. Later, when I woke, my snot-stained face and bruised body retold the story of my life in the real world.

Abuse became the norm. Whenever Dad struck me, I thought, *Here we go again. How long will it be until the next time?* Bruises, always covered by my *shalwar kamiz,* stippled my body. Once or twice, when I was getting changed for PE at school, Jane noticed. I told her I had fallen down the stairs. I was embarrassed and ashamed. I didn't want my best friend to ostracize me. I was lonely enough as it was—losing Jane would have been unbearable.

Dad was the *Imam.* The revered holy man. Who would have believed Mum if she said Dad was beating his five-year-old daughter? Even if they did, would they then conclude that Mum had shamed the family—and the entire community—by speaking out? It is considered better for a woman to suffer in silence, than to bring shame to her family or community. Anything is preferable to shame.

Even child abuse.

At first, Dad used my behavior — food prepared incorrectly, cleaning done incompletely — to instigate the beatings, but it wasn't long before his violence became capricious. As abusing his five-year-old daughter became habitual, Dad's mind began creeping into even darker places.

CHAPTER 5

Innocence Lost

❋

Children see people's skin color, but don't often judge them by it. My two white friends Jane and Susan had an amazing life. They told me about their holidays to the seaside, their trips abroad, and their visits to relatives in different parts of the country. They never seemed to get beaten by their parents or worry about bringing shame on the community. And they certainly didn't seem to spend their time second-guessing what the rules were. Jane and Susan didn't live in darkness and fear. I wanted to have their lives.

Their mum was forever inviting me to their house to play. But Mum always said that I wasn't allowed to go. She'd speak to me in Punjabi, telling me what I should say to their mum.

"Tell them you're sorry, but you can't go. Tell them it's because you have to cross a very dangerous road to get there."

"But I can go," I'd argue with her. "I *can* cross that road. Please let me go."

"No. It isn't possible. Now, just tell them what I told you."

I'd make my excuses, and Jane's mother would smile and say maybe next time. I knew Mum's real reason for not letting me go. If Dad knew I had been to visit my white friends, he'd be furious. No daughter of his would enter the home of people so dirty, godless, and immoral. If any one of us set foot in a *gora's* house, we could be contaminated and corrupted.

I didn't argue. But every week I told Mum I wanted to go to visit. Mum's response was always the same: *It wasn't allowed.* Of course, Jane and Susan kept inviting me. They could see no reason why they couldn't have their cute brown friend over to play.

"Come and play at our house!" Jane would say. "We've got Barbies and everything. And we can all get into our swimming stuff and go in the pool."

Swimming was absolutely out of the question. Swimming meant showing forbidden flesh — bare ankles, arms, and thighs. Dad wouldn't allow that, even though I was a small child. Swimming lessons had started at school, but my parents wrote a note saying I couldn't go. They said I didn't have a swimsuit, and I had problems with my hearing and couldn't get my ears wet.

The teachers didn't want me to be the odd one out, so they found me a swimsuit and a hat to protect my ears. But my parents reacted by insisting point blank that I wasn't allowed to swim. My teachers felt they couldn't go against them. When everyone else went to the pool, I sat alone in the classroom doing some coloring.

Of course, if I had gone swimming all my bruising would have shown. That was another, unspoken reason for my parents' prohibition. But as with everything in our lives, it was hidden under the cloak of being *haram*, forbidden. Who was going to challenge the *Imam's* version of what was and wasn't allowed? Other Muslim parents allowed their children to go swimming, which made me feel again that I was being punished by my father.

❋ ❋ ❋

Whenever Dad beat me, he ranted about how I was unwanted. He'd never wanted a daughter, he yelled, and I would never be good enough for his God, Allah. The gates of heaven would never open for a worthless girl like me. I was going straight to hell, he'd scream.

It turned out my father would take me there.

Six months after the first time Dad beat me, he stepped into my bedroom. He'd already beaten me that day, and I was lying on my bed, imagining the Lavender Fields. Dad *never* entered the women's bedroom. As the door creaked open, I shrank under the blanket in a desperate attempt to hide.

He stared at me, an expression of loathing mixed with something else on his bearded face. "You ... you're evil," he announced quietly. "You will surely burn in hell. But for now, your evil must be punished, driven out of you. Beating isn't enough."

He stepped toward me, murmuring over and over that I was a "dirty, worthless, temptress girl" and that he'd "never wanted a daughter." He stopped by the bed. I clamped my eyes shut, willing the Loneliness Birds to carry me away. I felt his hand pawing the blanket. My body tensed as he tugged my cover away.

As my father sexually molested me, he told me he was punishing me. It hurt physically, but not as much as the beatings. Yet it felt far worse emotionally. My terrified mind could not comprehend what was happening. All I knew was that it was wrong and dirty.

I accepted my "punishment." I was a confused and terrified little girl, and part of me still longed for my father's approval and love. I hated him for doing this to me, yet I wanted him to love me as a father should. Would acquiescing to his demands make him love me?

Finally Dad stood up from the bed. "You deserve everything you got," he sneered. "And if you ever tell anyone about your punishment, I will kill you. And then you'll go to hell, for Allah would never allow a dirty little girl like you to enter Paradise."

My father held total power over me, and he was intoxicated by it.

He left me on the bed, terrified and wracked with guilt and shame. I believed every word he told me.

The next week, the same thing happened. And the next week. And the week after that. I never knew exactly when it would happen, and I lived in a state of constant fear.

The first time Dad raped me, I felt as if I was going to die from the agony of his weight pushing down on me. I lied to Mum and told her I'd had a nosebleed — though how a nosebleed ended up bloodying the bed halfway down the sheets didn't seem to bother her. She simply scolded me for dirtying the bed and making more work for her.

Soon, the rapes became routine. Dad would take me into the bedroom for punishment, and I'd stare at the ceiling pretending it was happening to someone else. I'd pray for the Loneliness Birds to carry me away to where my rapist father couldn't touch me anymore.

You are evil, was my dad's constant refrain. *And this is the only way to drive the evil out of you.*

Each time he raped me, my feeling of dirtiness increased. I visited my Lavender Fields more and more frequently, but not even my fields could shield me from the horror and shame. I was worthless and sick to the core of my soul. I believed I deserved my punishment, and wondered if it would ever end.

Mum never once questioned my recurring nosebleed stories. Mum was unable to defend me when Dad beat me, and nothing had changed. She was unwilling — or perhaps unable — to face the truth. It would have been too shameful for her. She would rather have died.

I had no one to talk with or confess to. My family didn't care. I wasn't close to my teachers. I didn't trust any friends sufficiently. I was completely alone. And at almost six years old, I didn't have the words to explain, even had I wanted to.

I started to make up stories in my head. I imagined for myself a different life, hoping it might become real. I was a little white girl, living in Jane and Susan's house, playing happily in an entirely different life. In my mind, being white, living a normal life, and enjoying a loving family were inextricably linked. A Muslim Pakistani girl like me didn't have a chance.

I wrote my stories in a little notebook I kept hidden on top of the wardrobe. I wrote in English, so that even if my parents found my stories they wouldn't understand them. English was my secret language, and the language of the community I dreamed about joining. I escaped into life as a *gora*, for I could never imagine my father's horrors happening in Jane and Susan's world.

❋ ❋ ❋

I could do nothing to stop my father, and so I did as he demanded—no matter how sick and revolting it made me feel. It was a vicious cycle. The more I was abused, the dirtier and more deserving of such punishment I felt. The more my father abused me with impunity, the darker and more abusive his power trip became. In many Islamic societies, a victim of rape is often seen as the guilty party who has tempted the man into sexual excess. So it was with my father.

Eventually the hurried rapes in the bedroom no longer sated him. Or perhaps the bloodied sheets were becoming harder to explain away. Either way, Dad decided to take me to a new place of torture. At the back of the house, beneath the kitchen, was our cellar.

It became my hell for the next ten years.

Through a wooden door and down a flight of creaky wooden steps was a dark and damp cell, the size of a small, narrow bedroom. Bare brick walls. A bare brick floor. No light bulb, just a stained and half-rotten standard lamp casting a dim, eerie glow. The cellar wasn't used for anything much, and vermin scampered across the floor.

Dad would lock the door and do whatever he wanted to me, at his leisure and without the slightest danger of being disturbed.

My father began locking me in the cellar with no food or water. He kept me imprisoned for hours — sometimes even days — naked in the cold and damp. I would have nothing to keep me warm apart from the *shalwar kamiz* I had been wearing when he dragged me down to be punished.

"You! Don't you know no man will ever want you!" he kept taunting me. "You're disgusting and dirty. Look at you! You'll never be married because you are a useless, dirty, worthless girl."

When he was done raping me, he would leave me down there, alone and shivering in the suffocating dark. Mice and unseen things scuttled around me as I huddled against one brick wall. I hunched myself into a corner, wishing I was dead, and praying for the Loneliness Birds to come rescue me. I dreamed of them carrying me off to the Lavender Fields.

In my mind I was free, a happy white girl in the land of *goray*. We lived in castles surrounded by fields of lavender, and everything was happy and everything was good. But this magical world couldn't hold me forever, and eventually I would come to my senses. Those were the times I would wish for my life to end, and with it the darkness and suffering.

Sometimes Dad would lock me in the cellar before going to the mosque to preach. If he'd left the key in the outside of the door, Mum might bring me some food: a plate of curry with some *chapattis*. She stayed completely silent while she delivered it, wordlessly handing the plate to me. Sometimes I was only half dressed when I came up those creaking steps. She never looked at me. She couldn't acknowledge that her husband, the *Imam*, was abusing her six-year-old daughter.

Not once did I ask her to let me out; I knew that she was too scared. Once Dad caught her bringing me food, and he flew into a terrible rage, beating her savagely. As his fists pounded her, he screamed at Mum for interrupting his punishment. How could he cure my evil ways if his wife kept interfering? He was the master of this house, and he knew what his cursed daughter needed!

Mum was terrified. Several times she did take the risk of leaving the door unlocked so I could escape, hoping Dad would assume he hadn't trapped me properly.

Sometimes I was kept in the cellar for days on end. I'd

even miss school, but I'd just tell the teachers that I had been ill. I must have looked pale and sick and exhausted. None of my teachers ever questioned it, or seemed suspicious about what was really happening at home.

❀ ❀ ❀

Jane and Susan persisted in inviting me over to their house. They got their mother to help persuade Mum. "Hannan must come round to visit," their mother remarked to mine one day after school. "The girls are dying to have her over. We'd love to have her. Don't you think she might?"

Mum smiled and said, "Thank you." But she left it there. She avoided setting a date, or even giving a definite answer. Hiding behind her lack of English was the perfect excuse. I decided then to sneak off to their house. I knew where it was, because we walked past it on the way home from school. If I weren't gone for too long, Mum would assume I was playing at a friend's house somewhere on East Street.

One summer afternoon, I slipped out of the house without a word of explanation. I was always off at Amina's or another friend's, so I knew I wouldn't be missed. I made my way down East Street until I reached the main road. The cars zooming back and forth at breakneck speed scared me, so it took me several attempts before I finally plucked up the courage to dash across.

Jane and Susan lived in a big, modern-looking detached house. Whenever we walked past, I marveled at their front garden full of beautiful flowers. It reminded me of the Lavender Fields. I made my way along the path at the side of their house, and there were Jane and Susan, playing on the swings in the back garden. As soon as they caught sight of me, they started squealing with delight.

"You made it! Wow! Hannan's here!"

I could barely believe my eyes. Their back garden was magical, like something out of a fairy tale. The wide lawn was fringed with a riot of bright flowers. Chairs and a table were arranged around a small pond. Buckets and spades were scattered on the grass, and a paddling pool, complete with plastic ducks, finished the scene.

Jane and Susan grabbed me by the hands, grinning. They were dressed in skimpy Lycra shorts and tops. I felt so awkward in my hot, all-enveloping *shalwar kamiz*. Their mum was in the kitchen. From the open window she called out a jolly greeting and emerged with a plate of biscuits and glasses of fruit juice.

Then the sisters invited me in to see their rooms. Of course, their mum didn't mind one bit having me in their house. I was shocked to see that Jane and Susan each had their own room. A painted sign on each door announced "Jane's Room" and "Susan's Room." Inside each was a pine bed high enough so you could sit underneath — and that was where they stored their toys! I didn't have one single toy at home.

Each girl had a doll's house with a set of wooden furniture. My Little Pony dolls and Barbie dolls with lavish wardrobes lay everywhere. Jane, Susan, and I spent what seemed like hours dressing the Barbies, combing their hair, and driving them around in their cars. Then we each took turns combing our own hair: Susan's fire-red tresses, Jane's brunette locks, and my jet-black mane. Jane had a dressing table with plastic jewelry, hairbrushes, and flowered hair clips.

In no time two hours had flown by — two hours of illicit, forbidden pleasure. I started to worry about going home. If I was away for much longer, Mum was bound to start looking for me. It wouldn't take her long to discover I wasn't on our street. Reluctantly, I said my goodbyes to Jane and Susan, and their mum.

"Come again, any time," she told me. "It was lovely. You had such a nice time playing together. Promise you'll come."

"I promise," I murmured. "And thanks."

I didn't know if I would be able to keep that promise. With dragging feet I retraced my steps, hoping no one would see me. I slipped back unnoticed into my house, a place of darkness and foreboding after the light and joy of Jane and Susan's home.

"Where have you been?" were Mum's first words.

"Out playing on the street," I replied, as innocently as I could.

I avoided her eyes and busied myself in the kitchen with work I knew she had for me. Mum didn't ask any more questions. We never spoke much in any case, and she was used to my wandering. It was *leaving*—crossing the divide into the *goray's* territory—that was forbidden.

My visit to Jane and Susan's had been true rebellion. It felt frightening and dangerous, and I was relieved no one had caught me. It was also exciting, and somehow liberating. That evening, I thought to myself that it was good to have done it. It felt *good* to break the rules. It was my first secret rebellion, and I vowed there would be more.

In the days that followed, I reflected on the differences between my life and that of Jane and Susan. I thought of their toys, their separate rooms, and their magical playground in the back garden. Why was my life the way it was, and why was theirs that way?

Most of all I wondered why they had such a nice mum who took me into their home, when my white friends were banned from my house. She seemed so lovely; she laughed and chatted with her daughters as if they were friends. Jane and Susan had conversations with their parents, rather than merely receiving orders and abuse. Having seen their home, I knew I'd never let them into my house. I had nothing—*absolutely nothing*—for them to play with.

I could only conclude that this was my place in life. I was not a beloved daughter, like Jane and Susan. I wasn't an honored son, like my brothers. I was useless and shameful, only fit to be abused at Dad's whim.

I wanted Susan and Jane's life; I wanted to be white. In my mind, one came with the other. It wasn't about religion, but race. I longed for their parents, and their golden, sunlit lives.

Jane and Susan lived in the Lavender Fields — the happy, safe place of my dreams.

CHAPTER 6

Submission

❁

By the time I was six years old, Mum decided it was time for me to start doing the domestic chores. I had to cook, spending much of my time in our dismal, ocher kitchen. It had 1960s-style wooden laminate kitchen units, a red tiled floor, and a stainless steel sink. In one corner, a huge pipe ran down the wall. The one source of light was a bare bulb, hung from the ceiling.

The first time I cooked, Mum showed me how to slice the onion finely. It was the first time I'd handled a knife, and my hands were clumsy. I cut the onion into thickish slices and put them in the pan to fry with the oil and spices. Mum looked over to check what I was doing, then without warning she flew into a temper.

"Weren't you listening?" she cried. "Weren't you watching? The onions need to be smaller, just like I showed you! How can you be so stupid?"

I was shaken and shamed. I was used to such words from my father, but Mum had never spoken to me in such a way. Unlike Dad, Mum didn't actively *dislike* me. Normally, she seemed a kindly and well-meaning, though impotent, figure. But in the kitchen she was a tyrant. Even the smallest deviation from her way of doing things would earn me a scolding.

I cooked in fear. If Dad perceived one single thing as imperfect with his food, that was his excuse to fly into a raging fury. Mum feared that, and she transferred the terror to me. Her life with Dad was so abusive and dark, she had learned some of his abusive ways herself.

Whenever I did anything wrong in the kitchen, Mum assumed I had been daydreaming. In fact, I wasn't a natural cook. She liked *chapattis* to be perfectly round to fit on the plates, and I could never make them round enough. I'd take a lump of dough, ball it up, and roll it out flat with a rolling pin. But whereas Mum's were all perfect circles, mine were raggedy-edged and irregular.

Dad was forever ordering me to fetch him food and drink from the kitchen. He was even less happy with my cooking than he was with Mum's. No matter what I cooked — chicken, okra, or vegetable curry — he would declare it awful, and me useless. When my *chapattis* weren't perfectly round, he'd throw them back at me.

"What's this?" he'd yell. "Useless! Put it in the trash! I want round ones like your mother makes. Go and do it again. And you'd better get it right this time ... "

There was always the fear in my mind that he might beat me or drag me into the cellar. Things got worse after my sister, Sabina, became old enough to help in the kitchen. She was a natural cook who made perfect curries, just like Mum, and perfectly round *chapattis*.

Sabina would show off, singing out: "Look! Look at my round *chapattis*! Round — just like Dad loves them!" When she delivered them to my father, he would eat them with gusto.

I couldn't simply shrug it off, telling myself: *A round* chapatti *or a square one — what's the difference? Who cares?* I wanted to do it right. I wanted to please my father and be a proper Muslim girl. I wanted my father to be proud of me, and cooking food that he would love was part of this. My father's faith meant so much to him, I believed if I could be a good Muslim girl then I could please my father too. But I was never able to master it. The more Mum criticized me, the more nervous I became in the kitchen, forgetting to add salt or spices.

As for my brothers, they never commented on my food. They just ate it, their faces invariably glued to the television. Still, I was relieved they didn't abuse me and throw it back in my face. That was compliment enough for me.

❋ ❋ ❋

One afternoon when I was nearly seven, I was watching a children's cartoon. I laughed at one of the jokes, when suddenly I heard Dad's voice from the doorway. "Shut up!" he snapped. "I don't *ever* want to hear you laughing. I don't even want to see you smile. Or else."

I turned back to the television in fear. I knew if I

answered back I would be taken to the cellar. But in that instant I made a vow to myself: *I am going to laugh and smile. I'll never stop, no matter what you do to me.* I was determined not to let my father take it from me. It was a part of me I wouldn't let him violate or kill. Laughing gave me strength and courage. It added color to my soul that my father's dark desires could never fully overpower.

My father had already all but beaten the laughter out of my mother. I never saw her happy when he was around. But my schoolteachers often remarked that I was the easiest person to make laugh. I smiled so readily, like an eager puppy desperate for love and kindness.

Even something as commonplace as a school outing to Bermford Parish Church was a big deal for me. The church was cold and cavernous, almost like a cathedral, but the vicar was lovely—a warm, friendly man in his thirties who wore a black suit and white collar. He visited our school to help with the religion lessons, telling us Bible stories with words that painted vivid, life-like pictures.

I heard about baby Jesus, Joseph and his Technicolor dream coat, Moses and the burning bush, and Daniel in the lion's den. As the vicar talked, he drew cartoon-like pictures with colored pencils on a flip board. Sometimes, he even brought puppets who, with the help of student volunteers, acted out the Bible stories. His enthusiasm was infectious. I stayed in the back row, watching, but on the inside I was curiously attracted.

One day the vicar told us a story about Jesus. He

explained that Jesus was one of the prophets mentioned in the Qur'an alongside the prophet Mohammed. I was surprised. Dad had never mentioned Jesus before, and Dad knew the Qur'an backward and forward. I decided to tell Dad about my lesson — maybe he would be pleased I had learned about the Qur'an at school.

"The teacher told us Jesus is in the Qur'an," I ventured, hopefully, once Dad got home. Maybe for once he would be pleased with me. "He said — "

"Don't you ever mention *that man's* name in this house!" my father roared. "Never again! You hear me?"

I felt his knuckles against my face as he slapped me with the back of his hand. The stinging pain left me in no doubt that Jesus was also against the rules.

Later in life I would understand that Jesus is a major prophet in Islam. In the Qur'an he is known by the Arabic name of *Isa*. Perhaps Dad was ignorant of this fact, or perhaps he just hated the Christian version of the name. But I carried on smiling as the vicar told his stories. My father would never take my laughter.

I felt like a survivor. Dad took my innocence and my childhood. He abused and violated my body. He used his cruel words to try to cut my soul apart. But my laughter was my own.

※ ※ ※

One day I was grocery shopping in town with Raz and Mum. Just as we were about to enter the supermarket, a tall white man greeted us. He was wearing a white *jellabiya* (Muslim robe) and a *topi* (skullcap), the uniform worn by Arab men. On this *gora*—with his long beard, dyed red with henna, and his piercing blue eyes—it looked quite strange.

Raz greeted him with a manly hug, and I learned they knew each other from the mosque. This was the first white convert to Islam I'd ever seen. Raz was mightily pleased, but I was shocked. Dad had never mentioned a white convert at the mosque. I didn't even think white people were allowed there. I assumed they would be banned, as they were at home.

Anyway, why on earth would a white person want to leave *their* world and join *ours*? I longed for the exact opposite. Over time I learned that there were other converts who, whether white or black, were welcomed by most people, as long as they were coming to Islam. In fact, many people in our community had friends who were "outsiders." My uncles would talk openly about their *goray* friends. It was chiefly my father who seemed to hate all outsiders.

Dad didn't actively scold others in the community for having foreign friends. He simply ignored their relationships with these friends. In his mind there was a strict hierarchy: Pakistani Muslims, especially the holy men such as himself; Arab Muslims; other Asian Muslims—Indians, Bangladeshis, and so on; white converts; white unbelievers; and then black unbelievers. Most reviled were the Jews, because he believed they had taken the land from Muslims in Israel and Palestine.

In Saudi Arabia, the Muslim holy land, Pakistani Muslims are generally viewed as inferior because they are not Arabs. My father accepted his place in the pecking order. The Saudi Arabs were the direct descendants of the prophet Mohammed, and hence they were the most exalted. It was the way of the world.

On Friday, the Muslim holy day, my father spent his entire day at the mosque. Mum stayed at home to cook a special meal — delicately spiced rice pudding and *halvah*, an Arabic sweet made of crushed sesame seeds and honey. Friday was a day of bathing, of scenting the house with incense. Dad insisted his best clothes be laid out in the front room, immaculately clean and perfectly pressed.

Sometimes, a neighboring mosque invited a holy man, a *pir*, to give a lesson and to recite the Qur'an. Local mosques joined together to pay for the *pirs* to fly over from Pakistan or Saudi Arabia. Only the men attended these special lessons and recitals at the mosque.

We women contented ourselves with watching a video afterward. The presence of women in the mosque, even if fully shrouded in their *burkas*, might be unbearably enticing to the gathered men. Any hint of femininity might detract from the men's ability to concentrate on the Qur'an recital, so lessening their spiritual experience.

Each child in our community was assigned a *pir* who would pray for the child to be strong in his or her faith and to uphold the Five Pillars of Islam. Sometimes, the *pir* would visit the child's home, which was considered a great honor. Houses would be scrubbed from top to bottom, and a great celebration planned. Everyone wanted to touch the hand or robe of the visiting *pir*, almost as if they themselves were objects of veneration.

Pirs received cash donations from families. There was no set rate, but it was honorable to give as much as possible. Invariably, the *pirs* were far better off than the people to whom they ministered. They dressed in well-tailored clothes, and drove down East Street in sleek Mercedes cars. Any man could declare that he'd been called by God to be a *pir*, but not a woman, of course.

When I was seven years old, my *pir* came to visit me. He was Pakistani, but he lived in Saudi Arabia. When he arrived, he swept regally into the women's lounge. My father, plus a gaggle of women including my mum, my sister, and my aunties, came forward to greet him. The room quickly filled to overflowing with women, most of whom simply wanted to be in his presence and touch his robe.

He sat on the floor, and we immediately followed. My *pir* was wearing a heady, spicy oil, the scent of which overpowered my senses in the small room. Strict Muslims believe that one shouldn't use alcohol on the skin, as alcohol is *haram*. Instead, one uses *halal* aftershave, or scented oil, which is difficult to find in Britain.

As this was the first time I had met my *pir*, I was afraid he might tell me that I was evil, just as my father had always done. He was more holy than my father, so he would definitely think I was unworthy of heaven if my father thought that.

I was still reeling from the pungent smell, as my *pir* began to recite parts of the Qur'an, and I struggled to follow him, line by line. He told me I had to recite those verses every day. Then he gave my parents two gifts. The first was a *taviz*, which was a small metal locket to put around my neck, containing one handwritten verse of the Qur'an—as a *pir*, he was allowed to copy the scripture. The second gift was a verse written on a piece of paper. My parents were instructed to cut it up and stir it into my drink so that I would ingest the holy words.

The ceremony was complete. I met my *pir*, my spiritual guide, and my big day was done. Dad escorted my *pir* into the men's lounge for several hours of tea and conversation. I sought out my mum with my eyes. *What was all that about?*

Everyone had made such a big deal about this holy man coming to visit. I had been so looking forward to it. At last, my family was doing something to make me feel special. We were all wearing new clothes. For once, even I was dressed up. We had cleaned the whole of the house and cooked a feast—the sort of food we would never normally eat. Yet the *pir* had only been with me for two minutes, if that. I was relieved the visit with me was over, but I was also annoyed that even though he was *my pir*, I only got to see him for two minutes!

My *pir* decided to eat in the men's lounge, so I spent my time ferrying plates of sumptuous food from the kitchen. Each time I knocked on the door, one of my brothers took the plates from me before shutting the door in my face.

Once the men finished eating, I was allowed to eat with the women in the back lounge. I enjoyed the special food, but couldn't shake the feeling that it was all a scam. If that was the greatest treat my parents could manage for me in the first seven years of my life, then they could keep it. Give me Jane and Susan's Barbie dolls over meeting my *pir* any day of the week.

Later, my mum gave me the locket to wear, plus the Qur'an verse chopped into a glass of orange drink. I had to swallow the little pieces of paper along with the orange juice. If I had strained it out with my teeth, I'd have been in big trouble. As I drank the juice, I could feel the paper go down my throat, but I didn't notice any change in the way I felt about the Qur'an or prayer or anything else spiritual.

❈ ❈ ❈

If there was a highlight to life at the mosque, it was weddings. A wedding lasted for three days, and included a henna party, a register office signing, and two celebrations: the first at the groom's house and the second at the bride's house. Then the main ceremony took place at the mosque.

If we knew the family well, we were invited to the henna party. Using a tube of traditional, plant-based dye, painters produced complicated designs—swirls, fans, tendrils, buds, and delicate flowers—on the hands and feet of the participants. When the henna dried and cracked off, the women would be left with an intricate pattern of earthy red that could last for weeks. The henna parties also involved traditional Pakistani dancing —something similar to Bollywood dancing. It was very flirtatious, but of course we women only danced with other women!

At the mosque, men and women were separated for the wedding. The bride was allowed into the men's room, accompanied by her mother and aunts. She looked stunning in a pink *shalwar kamiz*—pink or red is the traditional color of Muslim bridal wear—and her jewelry glittered. Gold bracelets hung from her arms, gold necklaces looped her throat, and long gold earrings dangled from her ears. Crowning the splendor was a beautiful gold pendant, a *tika*, that fell on the center of her forehead.

The bride sat on a stage beside the groom, who dressed in a Western-style suit with a waistcoat. Dad read the wedding ceremony, while we women and girls, locked away from the proceedings in our room, gossiped among ourselves.

The bride was not supposed to smile or appear at all happy. If ever a bride looked remotely joyful, Dad scolded her. She was supposed to show sorrow at leaving her parents. Often, this wasn't difficult. Since the marriages were arranged, the bride was invariably nervous, if not downright terrified, about her new life. In some cases, she hadn't even met the groom before the wedding. The groom was allowed to be happy, although not required.

Dad asked each of them if they agreed to the marriage. Presuming they said yes—and woe to any who dithered or erred—Dad instructed them to recite a particular *surah* from the Qur'an. Following the ceremony, the men tucked into the wedding feast while the bride and groom remained sitting on their stage. When the men had finished, they went into a side room, and we women and girls were finally allowed in to eat.

During the feast, people approached the couple to give them gifts—clothes, items for the home, or envelopes full of money. Later, in the groom's house, the bride's parents placed a garland of money around the groom's neck, as part of the dowry they owed. The two sets of parents reached a private agreement before the wedding about how much the dowry should be. There was no set amount, but it usually included money, new clothes, and livestock for the extended family in Pakistan.

One reason girls are often so unwelcome in Pakistan is that it will cost their parents so much to marry them off. This is the curse of the dowry system. Dad frequently reminded me that he never wanted a daughter. Boys were celebrated and added wealth and honor to the family, while girls were merely an unwelcome burden—the least we could do was everything around the house! Parents thanked God for the birth of a baby boy, but a newborn girl was often met with silent regret.

One day I happened to see a television documentary about the treatment of girls in Asia. In India and Pakistan, female children were viewed as so costly to the family they were sometimes killed at birth. In my father's village, a girl being killed at birth would raise no eyebrows.

I had thought Dad was alone in his absolute hatred of women. But now the pieces began to fall into place. Our culture seemed predisposed to loathe and abuse women and girls. Part of me felt I should have been one of those girls murdered at birth. All surviving had achieved for me was to make me a victim of my father.

But not all fathers seemed restricted by cultural understanding of women and girls. There were other dads on the street who kicked a soccer ball with their sons or even held a skipping rope for their daughters. I'd seen Amina and Ruhama's father, Abdul, being lovely to them. He chased them in the park, laughing between the dark tree trunks, and he helped them with their homework.

Abdul even played with me if I was playing with his daughters. He cuddled and tickled Amina and Ruhama while they giggled happily. Abdul never hugged or tickled me, but he was always kind. At their house, he would smile at me and say, "Hello, Hannan! How are you? How are your parents?"

By contrast, my father never had a real conversation with any small child—even his own. When my brothers were old enough, he talked to them about mosque business or news from Pakistan or the Middle East. There was never any warmth or affection in his words. Dad never hugged anyone in his house.

The only physical contact from him came in the darkness of the nightmare.

CHAPTER 7

My Father's House

❀

I hear him before I see him.

I am lying on the cellar floor. The standard lamp lines each brick with an eerie halo. It is cold as the grave. The stairs creak, and fear grips my body. Snatches of mumbled Punjabi float into my darkness.

A splinter of hope. That he'll release me. That I'll be saved.

I hear shuffling sandals on the bare brick floor. He is moving toward me. I don't breathe. One, two, three, four . . . If I can reach 100 my father will think I am dead and leave me alone.

I want to be dead.

I try to be silent, unable to cry. I can't let him see my pain. He would love that. He would love to see my terror, to see his punishment working.

I am eight years old, and my father is coming to rape me.

❋ ❋ ❋

Whenever I emerged from the cellar, I felt defiled. I hung my head in shame, trying not to meet my mother's eyes. She buried herself in her work, clanging pans at the stove and bustling around the kitchen. It was her way of pretending that I wasn't there — of pretending the disheveled, filthy little girl standing in front of her hadn't just been raped by her husband.

"Can I go shower?" I mumbled, eventually.

I always felt I should apologize to Mum — for letting him do this to me, for not being good enough, for needing Dad to punish me again. I assumed Mum blamed me. But I could never find the right words. So, like Mum, I tried to ignore what happened, burying it so deep inside me no one would ever see it again.

I tried to act like everything was normal. What other option did I have?

"Can I go shower?" I asked again.

"If you need to," Mum replied without looking at me.

I turned away from her narrow, hunched back and headed for the stairs and the bathroom. I imagined my mother's shoulders shaking and trembling behind me, wracked with secret sobs. She really did care, I imagined, and what Dad was doing to me was splitting her heart.

I turned on the stairs.

Mum stood in the kitchen, composed and chopping onions. Not even onions made her cry.

As for Dad, he emerged from the cellar and changed

his *shalwar kamiz* for a fresh white one—one washed and perfectly ironed by Mum or me—before going to the mosque. Perhaps he thought Allah would absolve his sins. Perhaps he didn't think he'd sinned.

❋ ❋ ❋

When my father was abusing me, my brothers were often at home—but they spent their time watching soccer on television or listening to music in their rooms. As soon as they were old enough, they took weekend jobs at shops in town so they could get out of the house. When they weren't working, they were hanging out with their friends. These weren't options for me. I stayed at home with Mum, doing the chores and the will of the men.

Sometimes I risked complaining to my pampered brothers. "I'm not your slave," I'd say. "Go and do it yourself! You've got hands and feet, haven't you?"

Billy would try to talk me around. "But I'm tired, Hannan. *Please.*"

But Zakir and Raz would get angry if I didn't do exactly as they said, and they would threaten to tell Dad. Whenever they made that threat, I caved in right away. Dad would blow a fuse if I disobeyed any of his sons.

Occasionally, Billy tried to clear the plates from the table or wash the dishes. He used to speak to Mum and me in a gentle, kindly way. "Come on, Mum, you can't do the vacuuming *again*. Here, let me have a go." Mum tried to object. She didn't want Billy helping—she knew the rules of the house as well as I did. But sometimes,

Billy would insist, and Mum would be too tired to resist. If Dad found out, the punishment was swift.

My father encouraged the boys to do work fitting for a man: making the call to prayer on the loudspeaker system at the mosque.

> *Allah u Akbar, Allah u Akbar*
> *Ash-hadu al-la Ilaha ill Allah - Ash-hadu al-la*
>   *Ilaha ill Allah*
> *Ash-hadu anna Muhammadan Rasulullaah*
> *Ash-hadu anna Muhammadan Rasulullaah*
> *Hayya la-s-saleah - Hayya la-s-saleah*
> *Hayya la-l-faleah - Hayya la-l-faleah*
> *Allahu Akbar, Allahu Akbar*
> *La Ilaha ill Allah*

Which means:

> *Allah is most great (repeated four times)*
> *I bear witness that there is no other God but Allah*
>   *(repeated twice)*
> *I bear witness that Mohammed is the messenger*
>   *of Allah (repeated twice)*
> *Come to Prayer (repeated twice)*
> *Come to Success (repeated twice)*
> *Allah is most great (repeated twice)*
> *There is no God but Allah*

Billy hated speaking the call to prayer, and he refused to be totally cowed by my father. Whenever we had visitors, the men sat in the front room, but Billy tried to remain with the women. He hovered in the kitchen, talking to Mum and me as we worked and trying to lend a hand. Dad found this deeply insulting, since it shamed him in front of his friends.

With three brothers and my father to wait on hand and foot, my daily chores were endless. The worst job was washing the clothes. We hand washed everything in the kitchen sink, because we didn't have a washing machine. We used a big bar of green soap to lather the dirty clothes before rinsing them. We bleached the whites until they were white as snow.

I carried the baskets of washing out to the clothesline and helped fold the big sheets. I had to hide our bras and panties, so the men of the house couldn't see them. My brothers didn't care one way or the other about their little sisters' training bras, but Dad flew into a rage if any women's underwear was visible. It was fine for us to see his dirty underwear, of course, or my brothers', and to wash it by hand. But I hung our undies to dry in our bedroom, safely sequestered from my father's eyes.

Time taught me the harsh routine of my chores. On weekdays I was the first one up. I went downstairs and made traditional Pakistani tea, along with heaps of buttered toast. I took the tea and toast into the back lounge, opened a packet of custard cream biscuits, and arranged everything for my father and brothers.

After wolfing down my own breakfast alone, I stationed myself by the sink, washing up from the night before as quickly as I could. Then I'd rush to get myself and Sabina ready for school.

The threat of the abuse made me willing to do my chores—anything was better than the cellar. Even my little sister, Sabina, started to order me around. She watched the way the others behaved and followed their lead.

After school, Mum walked us home in time for our Qur'an lesson. Once that was over, I was allowed to watch television with tea and biscuits for half an hour. After that, I rushed through my homework before it was time to help with the evening meal. We ate dinner at eight, and then I cleaned until it was time for bed.

Saturday was the dreaded laundry day. By evening I was exhausted and retreated to my bed to read a library book by the light of the single bulb. I devoured books anytime I had the chance. I loved to reread books that our teachers read to us at school, because doing so reminded me of how happy I was away from the house. An adult dedicating time to read to me was a sign of real affection.

One of my most-loved books was called *Flat Stanley*, about a boy who gets accidentally flattened and then has all sorts of new and magical abilities as a flat person. But my absolute favorites were the *Please Mrs. Butler* poems, the best of which was called "A Dog in the Playground." The poems were so realistic, and were written in the way we would talk to each other at school. They spoke of life on the streets of my hometown, if not quite the reality of life on my street.

Once every two months Mum took us to the library in the town center where we were each allowed to choose five books. I started reading Judy Blume's Fudge books. Fudge was a bit of a loner, just like me. She lived in the United States, and her Americanisms—calling her mother "Mom," attending "first grade"—delighted me.

Despite my love of reading—or perhaps because of it—my parents didn't purchase me any books. With the exception of a Pakistani newspaper Dad read every day, and a handful of books on Islam and Pakistani history, our house held no reading material.

My father's mind still lived in his village in Pakistan. He never read anything about England—whether newspapers, magazines, or books—and tried to maintain a strict insularity.

After Saturday's laundry, Sunday was ironing day. I spent the day in the bedroom, ironing the clothes for our family of eight, while Mum cooked and cleaned downstairs. The boys' shirts, with their finicky collars, were the most difficult to manage. I could never get all the creases out, but at least I was left alone, able to retreat into my daydreams.

I'd listen to Top 40 hits on a small transistor radio. I'd gaze out over the terraces, my mind lost in a dream. Gradually, the neatly ironed clothes piled up on the bed. When I was done, I sorted the clothes and put them away neatly on the right shelves in each room.

I took special care with Dad's clothes. If I ironed them "badly," or put them back on his shelves "the wrong way," it was an excuse for him to punish me. As I worked, this threat was in the back of my mind, hanging over me like a dark and evil cloud, so I would daydream about my own little world of Loneliness Birds and Lavender Fields.

❊ ❊ ❊

As time passed it was more and more common for me to wake alone on the cold cellar floor. My family acted as if it were normal for me to be imprisoned. If it were a school day, Mum would get up early and make the breakfast instead of me. If it were a weekend and I missed my chores, I did the ironing during the week after school.

It was no secret Dad was punishing me, and there was no chance anyone would intervene.

School holidays were the worst. At least school gifted me a few hours when I didn't have to worry about Dad, but during holidays I had no escape. For weeks on end I was forced to stay in the house doing all the chores under the constant threat of punishment. Sabina was rarely made to help, and I felt like everyone's slave. A single mistake was sufficient reason for Dad to haul me into the cellar.

One day I put his ironed clothing in his room and went to the bathroom, seeking some small respite. Suddenly Dad barged in, locked the door, and ordered me to turn and face him. The bathroom was horribly cramped, and his body pushed me up against the toilet. "Remember," he hissed, his eyes dark pits of loathing, "I'll kill you if you ever breathe a word. You're dirty and worthless, and you're going to hell. That's all a cursed, evil *girl* like you deserves."

Once he was done with me, he shut the door and clumped down the stairs. I slumped over the washbasin and vomited, retching and retching until there was nothing left but bitter bile. Still the dirty, disgusting feelings lingered. I would never be clean.

After a year or two of the abuse, even Mum turned on me, telling me how worthless and useless I was. My father's sickness seemed to have infected the whole family but nobody would talk about it. My mum seemed to have accepted I was always going to take the punishment, because I deserved it. I knew other firstborn girls on my street were also made to help in the home. But they seemed so much freer and happier than me, with barely a fraction of the workload. And I couldn't imagine any of them being so horribly abused.

Even if they had been, who would have known?

※ ※ ※

Our family survived on donations to the mosque and the generosity of British taxpayers. Dad was on income support and Housing Benefit. Dad had managed to claim welfare by claiming to be unemployed, but of course he wasn't. Dad was the community's full-time *Imam*, and he did get paid, from the cash donations to the mosque.

Every aspect of my father's life — the food he ate, the

heating that warmed his home, his children's education and healthcare, the very water he drank—all of it was funded by the British state. And it was that same British state that he in turn abhorred, and attempted to ensure that his children abhorred, by bringing them up with the same attitudes and blind prejudices that he had.

It was only my father who seemed to believe that he had a God-given right to avoid normal responsibilities. The other men on our street worked and paid taxes. Some owned businesses. One man ran a *halal* dairy farm, selling eggs and milk to shops around town. Amina's dad, Abdul, was a hard-working bus driver.

My dad's decision to lie to the English government wasn't dishonorable in our community, although being caught would have been. Honor wasn't about what you *did* as much as what you were *seen* doing. If Dad had been caught, even then he might well have argued that taking what he could from the immoral land of *goray* was justified. And who in the community would have gone against him? Dad was unassailably honorable.

Indeed, in my father's mind, there may have been nothing wrong with locking his young daughter in the cellar and beating and raping her. As long as no one outside the family knew about it, it would not dishonor the family, the community, or the mosque.

My father believed he ought only to concern himself with matters of the spirit. He was above earthly worries and laws. Others accepted this for a variety of reasons.

Dad became above reproach, whether lying to the government, beating his wife, or raping his daughter.

❈ ❈ ❈

By the time I was ten, I had learned to read the entire 600-page Qur'an. Most Muslim children don't manage this until they are much older. I was so excited as I read the last few words of the final *surah*. I had seen the parties we had in the community when children finished the Qur'an. The child was given money and lots of sweets. I thought my parents had even more cause to celebrate, throwing a large party for the whole community.

As I walked to the door of the men's lounge to tell my father I had finished, I expected him to be delighted and, for the first time, proud of me. I struggled to read the whole Qur'an to please my parents. Part of me still hoped to win Dad's recognition and affection. I longed to prove I wasn't a cursed, worthless, evil girl. *See, Dad, I'm good, I'm good—I can read the entire Qur'an!* When I went into the room and told my father that I had finished, he didn't even look up at me from his book. I was defeated! There would be no celebrations and no gifts of money or sweets for my achievement.

CHAPTER 8

A Caged Bird
Crying

❋

I was eleven, and secondary school was right around the corner. My final primary school report was a mix of B's and C's. Billy read the report to Mum, going through it subject by subject. Mum congratulated me for once, saying how well I'd done for a girl. Unsurprisingly, Dad ignored it.

My results weren't exceptional, but between the domestic drudgery and the nightmare of the abuse, I was happy and proud to have done as well as I had.

My parents wanted me to go to a Muslim girls' school to safeguard my honor, which would be insulated from the evils of British middle school society, like smoking, drinking, and boys. Dad believed mainstream schools were dens of iniquity. But the Muslim school required fees, and my parents' poverty ensured I would attend a secular school.

Since I now associated my religion with submission,

pain, and suffering, I welcomed the news. By default, I ended up at Bermford Comprehensive, which was famous for being the worst school in town. The pupils were all locals, working class and impoverished. Crime was high in the area, and a good number of the local families were in trouble with the police.

My junior school was run by the Church of England, but it wasn't an issue for my parents. Every year I had gone to Bermford Parish Church for Easter and Christmas. But now that I was almost eleven years old—and approaching marriageable age—Dad wanted control over my schooling. He was becoming increasingly authoritarian with all of his daughters. Aliya attended the same Church of England school I had, and she came home telling stories about the vicar's exciting talks about Jesus and Christianity.

That was enough! Dad didn't shout at Aliya, but he was enraged that she was being exposed to all this Christianity, and he quickly alerted the community to the danger of their children being indoctrinated. Many East Street parents complained to the school, which relented in part, allowing Muslim children to stay in the classroom and color during church visits after that.

I quickly made new friends at Bermford Comp—including Iram, Karen, Amanda, and Lara. Iram was a Pakistani Muslim girl, and my only Muslim friend at school. She lived across town. Karen was striking, with red hair, a petite stature, and snowy white skin. Amanda was very beautiful, with lustrous brown hair and deep hazel eyes. But it was my English friend Lara who was the real belle of the bunch. She was tall, with coal-dark hair cut boyishly short, and smoldering, laughter-filled eyes. All the boys fancied Lara.

Lara was my best friend and protector. Under her influence, the other girls did their best to make me feel like one of them. Lara and the girls would share everything they did on the weekend with me, just as they did with other girl friends — even though they knew my weekend activities were very different from theirs.

But I could never quite forget I was an outsider. One day Karen and I were waiting at the bus stop outside the school gates when a car pulled up. Her father put his window down and yelled at Karen, "Get in the car! Just get in! What're you doing standing there talking to that bloody *Paki*?"

Karen didn't know what to say or where to look. She blurted a goodbye, jumped into her father's car, and squealed away. When I saw her the next day she looked mortified. Karen was a good friend, and I didn't want to make it an issue. In unspoken agreement, neither of us mentioned it after that, but she never waited with me again after school.

I knew my dad hated white people, and now I'd met a white person who hated me. Why was it always the adults who showed such blind hatred, while we children did our best to get along?

Amanda seemed to have everything: beauty, a winning personality, and a lovely family. Her house was near school, and sometimes we'd go there for lunch. Her father was a businessman and her mother was a housewife. Amanda seemed able to tell her mum anything, and her father supported and encouraged her.

I longed for Amanda's life. It wasn't her good looks I coveted. I wasn't bothered about being popular with the boys. I simply wanted the love and stability of a normal healthy family. If Amanda's parents had offered me a home, I would have ditched my parents without a second thought.

Toward the end of my first term, I arranged to meet Amanda in the town center. It was lunchtime on a Saturday, a time when I knew Dad would be at the mosque. Feeling brave, I invited Amanda to my house to hang out. I had never in my life invited a friend into my home, and I knew it was risky.

The front door was always unlocked, so we walked right in. I took Amanda into the lounge. We sat on the sofa and started talking. Mum brought us a drink and some biscuits, and I began to relax when suddenly the door opened and in walked my father. I froze as he caught sight of Amanda. An instant later he was standing at the open door, ordering me out of the room. I knew what was coming. He closed the door roughly behind me and started yelling at me in Punjabi.

"How dare you bring that *gori* here! In my house! How many times do I have to tell you? They're dirty infidels. They sleep around! They have no belief! They can't ... "

On and on he ranted. I'd heard this a thousand times before.

"I don't want her in my house!" he shouted. "And I won't have you having *gori* friends!"

When Dad started ranting, there was no point in chancing a reply. I hung my head and hoped Amanda wouldn't understand what he was saying. Suddenly, Dad stalked off to the men's lounge. Burning up with shame and embarrassment, I went back to Amanda.

"I'm really sorry," I muttered. "Dad says I have to go and pray. Is it okay if you leave now?"

"Of course," said Amanda. She jumped up and gave me a big hug, seeing how upset I was. "Don't worry. Enjoy your prayers, and I'll see you at school."

On Monday I apologized to Amanda for making her leave so soon. I tried explaining to her that Dad didn't like English people because he didn't understand them. It was the best excuse that I could think of.

Amanda gave a knowing smile. "I thought he had some sort of issue with me. He did seem very angry ... I hope I didn't cause you any trouble. But we were having such a nice time, weren't we? Pity he had to go and spoil it."

"It's not you," I tried to say. "Really it's not. So please, don't feel bad about it. My dad is the problem, not you!"

My apology didn't lessen my sense of shame. Amanda's parents had been so lovely to me, and *this* was how my father treated her? Why was I always the weirdo with the nasty family?

I wanted to tell my friends as much of the truth as I could. I wanted them to understand that I came from a place so different from theirs, it might as well be another planet. I wanted them to know that my father's hatred and hostility hadn't transferred to my generation.

But I couldn't simply tell Amanda that my racist dad hated white people. I didn't want her to feel like she had done anything to deserve his vitriol. I used my culture as a smoke screen to hide Dad's faults and to save Amanda's feelings.

If only what Amanda had seen were the worst of my father's behavior.

❊ ❊ ❊

At school we had to wear a navy blue skirt and white shirt with a navy blazer. My skirt fell just below my knees, but that wasn't enough for my father. Beneath it I had to wear navy cotton pants, *shalwar kamiz* style.

"Why do you have those weird pants on?" one of the other students asked.

I shrugged, resignedly. "I'm not allowed to show my legs." It sounded even stupider once I said it out loud than it sounded in my head.

"Not allowed to show your legs? Why not? What's wrong with them?"

"Nothing," I'd mutter. "It's because of my religion."

That was a conversation stopper—religion wasn't our main topic in school!

I was approaching the age of puberty, and this drove

my father's paranoia. When a Muslim girl from our community starts her period, she is barred from the mosque, from touching the Qur'an, and from praying at home. The Qur'an is quite clear that menstruation is an "indisposition" and that menstruating women are "unclean."[3]

Puberty meant new taboos at home. Mum had never told me that I would start my period. The sex education lessons at school didn't tell me where to get tampons or towels. Fortunately, a kind school nurse explained everything to me and gave me a few packs of free sanitary towels.

I was the first among my school friends to start my period. They were keen to know just how it felt, which gave me a brief spell of unexpected popularity. At home, however, it was different. Because menstruating women are viewed as unclean, I associated my menstruation with sin. I didn't tell Mum for months. Eventually I ran out of sanitary towels, so I had to confess what was happening.

Mum told me I was not to use tampons because putting something unnatural into my body was wrong. She admonished me not to pray when I had my period—finally, a religious rule I was happy to follow!

Dad didn't realize I had started menstruating for a year or more. He was used to me bleeding whenever he sexually assaulted me. However, once he understood, he avoided raping me during my period, when I was too unclean for him to touch. Other girls at school moaned about their periods, but for me it was a blessed release.

During that first year of secondary school, Dad was

raping me in the cellar at least once a month. My new, more mature group of friends started to notice my bruising. It must have been obvious that all wasn't right, especially when we changed for PE. I'd have bruising around my breasts, where he'd been groping me, and around my thighs. But no one ever challenged me to explain it, and I had no desire to reveal what was happening. If Dad had been doing this to my sisters, I would have known straight away it was wrong. But not when he was doing it to me. I had started to believe I deserved the punishment.

I began to think about escape. The only way out I could see was to attend college or university—either that or kill myself. I considered running away from home, but the only people I knew well were Muslims who would take me back to my father. There was no way I could tell them what was happening. They just wouldn't believe such a thing of their *Imam*.

I lived for the dream of escape, which drove my studies in school. If I studied hard, I might win a place to go to sixth form college (two additional years at secondary school) or university. I knew of girls in our community who had left home to do further studies. I knew that would give me a way out, for then Dad would have no access to me. It was the only sure route of escape I could see.

But I was far from sure if my parents would even allow me to leave, and I was only an eleven-year-old girl. College was six years away.

❈ ❈ ❈

That summer I was overjoyed when my father decided to spend the holidays in Pakistan. For me it meant several weeks of blessed release, but it meant something very different for my brother. Raz was sixteen years old, and my father took him to Pakistan to enter a *madrassa* to become a *hafiz*, a man who has learned the Qur'an by heart. After three years, Raz would be able to quote any verse of it in Arabic from memory, ensuring him a place of honor in any Muslim community.

Dad took Raz without telling us that he wasn't coming back.

Raz was a gentle, simple soul. I was sad to see him go, and worried. I wondered how he would fare in Pakistan. My own Qur'an studies had been so hateful that I couldn't imagine what it would be like to be forced to learn every scripture by rote, especially in an alien language. From the beating that I'd experienced myself in the mosque, I couldn't imagine this Pakistani *madrassa* would be a healthy learning environment. In my mind, it was a place of brutality and violence.

There were one or two people in our community who were *hafiz* of the Qur'an. They recited the Qur'an at special times like *Ramadan*. It was a mark of great status in our community — status that my father, the *Imam*, no doubt coveted. It was via Raz that he aimed to achieve this honor, through my brother Raz whom I wouldn't see for another three years.

❋ ❋ ❋

Bermford Comp's field hockey team led the league for two years running, and I was one of the key players. I was fearless. I loved bashing the ball and shoulder checking the girls from the opposing team. The hockey pitch was my place to work out my pent-up aggression and internalized pain.

I loved being part of a team, especially since Lara played alongside me. Because we were on a winning streak, we shared a lot of laughter and celebration. It felt wonderful to excel, and leave myself for an afternoon.

But one day the inevitable happened: in the shower after a game, Lara noticed my chest was covered in bruises. She reached out her hand in involuntary alarm, then pulled it back to her face in horror. Her eyes met mine, wide with concern. She gestured at the appalling black and blue marks that lay beneath my flesh.

"What happened?" she gasped. "Surely that's not from the hockey ...?"

I shook my head.

I wished the shower water would wash me away, as I felt so ashamed she had seen.

"So how did ... did someone ... I mean, who did it to you?"

"I fell down."

I reached for the soap, hiding my eyes from Lara as I did so. "I fell, that's all."

"How did you fall and only hurt your boobs?"

I shrugged. "I dunno. I just fell down the stairs."

Lara stared at me for a few seconds, and then turned away. I felt dirty. I scrubbed at my skin with the soap, imagining I could smell my father on me. But no matter how hard I scrubbed, I couldn't get clean. I had lied to my best friend. I couldn't bring myself to tell her the bruises were marks of my father's groping fingers, as he locked me in the cellar and raped me.

As I peddled those lies and saw the doubt in Lara's eyes, I felt like a fraud. Standing in the school shower, scrubbing my skin until it became raw, I understood that my body and my life were no longer my own.

I was owned by my father.

CHAPTER 9

Rebellion's Spring

I still read my Qur'an most days before I went to sleep. I didn't understand the Arabic words, but it had been drilled into me that simply saying them was a virtuous act. Part of me was still trying to earn my father's affection, yet at the same time I understood that Dad was using his religion to justify his ongoing abuse.

When I read the Qur'an, I prayed for my life to get better, but it never did. So I began praying for my father to die. I knew it was sinful, but that didn't stop me. Everything painful in my life flowed from him. If he was dead, life was bound to get better.

So I prayed to Allah to take Dad's life. I didn't really think it would happen, but it helped me deal with my anger. In any case, my prayers were never answered. I began to think that God—my *father's* God—wasn't listening. I began to think that my father's God, Allah, was cruel and avenging, his heart devoid of love or happiness. Increasingly, I saw Allah in the image of my father. Allah threw people into the fires of hell and hung them up by their hair—at least according to my father. I lived in fear of Allah and his earthly agents: my mother and my father. I was aware, from the stories I had been told by the vicar in junior school, that Christians believed in a God who was loving and caring, and I thought the Christian God must be different from Allah. I was confused about the character of God, which was the beginning of my search for understanding and my questions about Islam.

❋ ❋ ❋

By now I was twelve and had a new best friend. Everyone knew her by her nickname "Skip," and she was a Muslim Pakistani five years my senior. I admired Skip because of her courage, honesty, and self-confidence. She was a tomboy and a born rebel. We spent our time kicking around a soccer ball in her backyard and laughing happily. If Dad caught us, he'd get really annoyed with us. Playing soccer was shameful, he'd rant—we ought to be inside, cooking and cleaning for the men-folk. Once Dad was gone, Skip would roll her eyes and ape my father's lecture, complete with waving arms and wagging eyebrows. To Skip, Dad was a throwback to a dark past.

Skip's greatest worry was that her father would force her into an arranged marriage. He was more of a businessman than a man of religion, but that didn't mean a forced marriage was out of the question. Such marriages weren't all about religion, they were about culture and tradition too. And, of course, honor.

Skip and I were forever discussing the forced marriages other girls in the street had suffered. Skip was the sort who wouldn't be forced into anything. She wanted to fall in love and marry for love. We used to fantasize about finding the perfect man and about the perfect wedding. Skip and I shared a dream of getting an education—she longed to free herself from the control of the East Street Muslim community, while I longed to escape from the darkness of my home.

Toward the end of our first year of friendship, Skip told me she was going on holiday to Pakistan. Two days after Skip left for Pakistan, our phone rang. "Hi, Skip, how are—?"

"Hannan? Hannan? Thank God you're there," Skip cut in, her voice cracking with tension and fear. "Listen, I need your help. I've got to be quick. If they catch me on the phone ..."

Skip told me how she had been taken to visit some distant relatives in northeast Pakistan. Upon arriving at the village, she had been presented to a Pakistani man—a cousin she'd never met—and told this was the man she was going to marry.

Skip was locked alone in a dark room with no food or water until she agreed to go through with the marriage. Rather than starve or die of thirst, she had consented. Soon after being released, she managed to get to a phone and was calling me out of sheer desperation. She was determined to escape. She needed me to speak to her older sister, Saira, and, most of all, she needed a flight out of Pakistan.

I hurried over to Saira's place. If my father found out I was helping Skip escape a forced marriage, I would be punished terribly. I would be rebelling against everything he valued. But I didn't care. I had to help Skip. Besides, what could he do to me that was worse than the punishments he already visited on me? It seemed only killing me could up the ante.

Saira was cut from the same cloth as Skip, and upon hearing my tale she leapt into action. That very day she got a ticket in Skip's name and arranged for a friend to hand carry it to Pakistan.

Three days later I got a call from Saira. Skip had escaped! She was safely back in the UK, staying at Saira's place and recuperating from her hideous ordeal. Amazingly, her fiancé had given back her passport and driven her to the airport. Without his help, she might not have made it.

Skip was shaken and shocked. She vowed never to speak to her parents again. She started working, rented her own apartment, and cut herself off from them completely. As far as Skip's parents were concerned, her actions had deeply dishonored the family, so they didn't want any contact with her, either.

Everyone on our street knew what Skip had done. She was in absolute disgrace, they said. She had brought such a deep shame on her family. My father was especially vehement in his condemnation. He was gripped by a dark fury. How could a girl from his street, one of his flock, so defy her father's will? The dishonor was felt by the entire community, but especially by him, the *Imam*.

I kept quiet about my role in her escape. We stayed in contact as best we could. Skip loved to travel. Every now and then she'd call me from Egypt or Israel or some other place. There was no real danger in her calling. All she had to do was speak in English, and Mum would hand the phone to me.

"English-speaking girl," she'd mutter in Punjabi.

✳ ✳ ✳

Skip's rebellion fuelled my own, although my actions at twelve were less decisive. My hair was long and cut to the same length, and every day I wore it in a thick braid. Several of the girls on my street had their hair cut into bangs, and I thought it looked great, but Mum told me Allah would punish them. Having bangs was *haram*, she said.

The way Mum and Dad talked, *everything* was *haram* — it was surprising that breathing was allowed! I thought bangs looked too fashionable to resist, so I decided to cut my own. I would simply have to keep it secret. Since I always wore a *hijab* over my head, even at home, I'd just make sure my forbidden bangs were never visible.

One evening after school, I went into the bathroom and locked the door. Many Muslims don't like to soak in a bath, because it's unclean to lie in water you've already dirtied. But it's not considered right to stand up to wash, either, so showering isn't allowed. I didn't understand why, I just assumed this was another rule in the Qur'an. Instead, we filled a yellow plastic bucket and, as we crouched in the bath, scooped water to pour over ourselves.

I readied the yellow bucket to collect my hair. I peered into the wooden framed mirror sitting over the sink and, taking the pair of pink-handled scissors I kept in my school pencil case, I cut a lock of hair. *Snip* — the strand came away so easily! I dropped it into the bucket where it landed soundlessly. The thrill of rebellion felt so liberating.

Snip, snip, snip ... until finally I was done. I picked up the bucket, up-ended it over the toilet, and flushed away the evidence. Then I started to feel worried and nervous. Would Mum notice? I fiddled with my *hijab*, pulling it lower at the front. When I opened the door and sneaked out of the bathroom, I joined Mum in the kitchen. She didn't so much as glance at me. Why should she? With my forbidden bangs hidden by the scarf, I looked exactly the same as before.

Some weeks later, however, I was taking off my *hijab* before bed when Mum walked in. I tried to turn away but it was too late — she'd already caught sight of my do-it-yourself hair.

"You stupid, stupid girl!" she cried. "What have you done? Stupid girl. So worthless and stupid!"

She strode across the room and slapped me hard across my face.

"For doing that, don't you know you'll be hung up by your hair in hell!" she cried. "You'll burn in hell for it!"

I was shocked into silence. Mum had never hit me before. Cutting my hair was wrong, but not *that* wrong, was it? When she cursed me, I feared her curse might come true. Yet at the same time, I struggled to understand how the simple act of cutting my hair could be so sinful. What real harm had I done? What kind of God could possibly be offended by that?

I reckoned I was going to hell anyway. A Muslim is supposed to adhere to the Five Pillars of Islam in order to reach Paradise, and I was already failing in that by sneaking off to watch British soap operas instead of praying five times a day. It looked as if mine was a lost cause, haircut or no haircut.

❋ ❋ ❋

Raz was still incommunicado at the Pakistani *madrassa*, but Zakir and Billy, now teenagers, were starting their own small rebellions at home. We were supposed to pray each night around the same time our favorite television soap *Neighbors* aired.

My brothers and I trooped upstairs, as if we were off to pray, and piled into Zakir's room for the latest episode. If either brother complained about having me in the room, I would threaten to tell Mum that they were watching television instead of praying.

At first, I watched *Neighbors* instead of praying simply because it was so much more interesting and fun. But by the time I was well into my secondary school I had learned enough about other religions to begin questioning my own family's faith system. It was at this point that I first began to question whether or not I actually wanted to be a Muslim. But as far as I could see, I was stuck in a religious ghetto, by birth and upbringing.

Dad got most of his sense of British culture from what we watched on television. If the characters were drinking alcohol in a pub and flirting, he'd remark, "Typical *goray!* That's all those English people ever do—drink alcohol and sleep around!" Since he had no direct experience of English culture, he believed all *goray* behaved like that. If young characters talked back to their elders, he found further proof there was no respect in English society.

Dad took joy in anything that reinforced his prejudices. He paid special attention to the news whenever it was about youth crime or underage drinking. What was even worse were scantily clad women on television, and if people were shown kissing, Dad would blow a fuse. He'd shout at us to turn to another channel immediately.

The more he disapproved, the more my brothers and I avidly watched the soaps. They were a window into a different world. But in spite of Dad's fears, we didn't want to be like the characters in the soaps. I watched those soaps because I wanted to be a part of my friends' world. Soaps were the one thing I could talk to my friends about that we shared—holidaying, boyfriends, clothes, hairstyles, and makeup were all forbidden for me. Television was our common ground.

Whenever Dad made us turn off an important scene, I knew I would feel left out at school the next day.

"You see *EastEnders* last night?" Lara would remark. "Wow! Who'd have thought *they* were having an *affair*?"

Karen would laugh. "Yeah, juicy, eh?"

"Who's having an affair?" I'd ask, eager to know the details I'd been forced to miss.

"You didn't watch it?" Karen would reply.

"I did, but not that bit."

Karen would look confused. "But why d'you always miss the best bits?"

"I'm not allowed to watch them!" I'd answer angrily. "My stupid dad won't let me."

"But why not?" Lara would ask. "What's wrong with it?"

"It's all about religion," I'd mutter, feeling utterly stupid to have to admit to such a thing. "He says it's un-Islamic to see them."

"But it's only kissing and stuff," Karen would interject. "They don't really *do* anything ..."

Then, in an another attempt to build a bridge with my school friends, I got into pop music. Inevitably, this caused me trouble at home. The television charts program *Top of the Pops* was Dad's *bête noire*, the show he reviled most. We children weren't allowed to listen to music; it was *haram*. Mum still listened to her Bollywood tapes, and Dad had his tapes of Pakistani *qawwali*, a type of music similar to the popular chanting whirling dervishes dance to in Pakistan. But when it came to *Top of the Pops*, Dad hated the music, the lyrics, the way people dressed, and the way they danced provocatively. *But,* I asked myself over and over, *how can singing and dancing be so sinful, but my father is allowed to abuse me in the cellar?* I didn't have everything figured out, but I knew Dad's moral compass was warped.

I kept watching *Top of the Pops*, especially if Dad was out. I tried to learn the lyrics to the hit songs, so I could sing along with my friends. Mostly, they were about romantic love between a man and a woman. Romantic love seemed thrilling and mysterious, so wild and free compared to my parents' sterile and abusive coupling. I never once saw my father treat my mother with one iota of affection or appreciation. In his eyes, she was no better than a multi-function domestic appliance.

When I looked at my parents, I saw nothing that spoke of love—not even the occasional soft word. Dad treated Mum like a slave. Instinctively, I knew this was wrong. I knew, in my heart, he should cherish her. She was his wife, his partner, the mother of his children. All he gave her was scorn and violence.

I told myself I didn't want to end up like Mum. But I saw older cousins and friends getting corralled into marriages that were equally loveless and stark. They didn't seem even slightly happy or in love. There was little I could see that testified to marital love in our community. Although I wasn't privy to what went on in every family's home, I never saw men and women showing any affection in public. No touching of any sort was allowed.

Even though they knew music was forbidden, Zakir and Billy were great fans of The Smiths and Morrissey. They'd listen late at night or when Dad was at the mosque. Both of them had stickers on their wardrobes of Morrissey, and one day they decided to gel their hair into quiffs, with a big curl in the middle of their foreheads, like their pop idols.

The first time they came downstairs with quiffs, Dad looked at them strangely, but he didn't say anything. My brothers kept on gelling their hair, and eventually Dad couldn't ignore it any longer. He didn't recognize that they were idolizing a rock star, but he sensed his off-spring being polluted with cursed Western ways.

"What's that all about?" Dad snapped, jabbing a finger in the direction of Zakir's quiff. "Long hair like a girl! It just looks stupid. So why do it?"

"It's nothing," Zakir muttered. "I just like it that way."

"Well, it looks stupid," Dad retorted. "*Gora* hairstyles —what rubbish!"

In Dad's opinion, the quiffs were a dangerous provocation. It was one step away from having long hair, which he hated. In his view, males ought to have close-cut hair in accordance with Islamic tradition. Huge, bushy beards were a definite yes, but long hair was a no-no.

Morrissey was a vegetarian and had a song called "Meat is Murder." It was one of my brothers' favorites.

Their next step in trying to be like him was to stop eating meat. One day they told Mum they had become vegetarians. She started making them separate meals, or she just served them the vegetables. For a few weeks Dad seemed oblivious. But eventually—just as with the quiffs—Dad couldn't ignore what was going on.

"What's all this—not eating your meat?" he snorted. "You'll never put on any weight or grow any muscles that way. How can you ever expect to be men?"

"What do you care?" retorted Billy, without thinking. "We just don't want to eat it, that's all."

Dad was furious, but he couldn't force his sons to eat meat. There was no way he was ever going to understand that they wanted to be vegetarians. It was another wedge of mutual incomprehension between my father and his sons.

I thought my brothers' veggie act was quite funny, even though I figured they were just being trendy. Soon they refused to eat any eggs that weren't free range, and Mum, who would do anything for her sons, changed her shopping habits. The rest of us teased Billy and Zakir mercilessly. We'd sit at the dinner table and select juicy chunks of chicken from our curry. My little sister loved to put the meat right under their noses.

"Mmm, doesn't that smell good?" she'd taunt them.

Mum's lamb *sag*—lamb and spinach curry—had always been Zakir's favorite. He especially liked it the second day after it had been cooked, in a toasted sandwich, when the spices had time to marinate. So we started eating lamb *sag* toasted sandwiches right in front of Zakir, just to wind him up.

"It's so tender! And the spices—mmm, perfect!"

Of course, Dad failed to see the humor. He ate in silence, thankfully unaware his sons' vegetarianism was inspired by a white rock star. As it was, he suffered his sons' aberrant behavior in a scowling, silent rage.

I couldn't rebel like my brothers. The threat of physical punishment kept me relatively cowed. I didn't try vegetarianism, and I always kept my tape cassettes of pop music well hidden in my bedroom. Though by now there were four of us sleeping in one room: Mum, Sabina, Aliya, and me. We each had one shelf in the wardrobe for our clothes. There were no posters or pictures on the walls, just more 1970s-style flowered wallpaper, same as the lounge.

In such close quarters, it became increasingly difficult to hide even the smallest rebellion from Sabina. If she found something out, she told my parents right away. We were like chalk and cheese, and we just didn't get along. She was Dad's perfect daughter, while I was the rebellious, cursed one—the one who deserved only his abuse and rage.

I had a school pencil case on which I had written my friends' names. Hidden inside were stickers of pop stars and actors from *Smash Hits* magazine like Bros, New Kids on the Block, and the stars of the television series *Beverly Hills 90210*. I would certainly have accepted an arranged marriage—with Luke Perry!

My parents never went through my school stuff, so my stickers were safe. But one time Sabina got a hold of my school bag and caused havoc. She ripped out and defaced all my stickers. My school bag was the entirety of my private life, and I had to defend it against everyone. I was livid. How could she *do* that? It was my only spot of privacy, and now everybody knew about it.

Another time Zakir and Billy got hold of my pencil case. They thought it was hilarious. Bros were a cheesy pop band for little girls, and they thought I was really sad for liking them. They laughed at me for trying to hide the stickers, and told me to stop being such a girl. Then they teased me about my crush on Luke Perry for weeks on end.

I was so angry with them. "What are you looking at? It's secret! Who said you could go in my bag?"

The more annoyed I got, the more it egged them on to jeer and laugh at me. But at least I knew they wouldn't tell Dad. We all had our secrets, and in a way we protected each other.

CHAPTER 10

Resistance, Sweet Resistance

❊

At thirteen I began to question my world. Why was my life so abusive and dark? Why was my spirit crushed by drudgery? The pillars of my life — my culture, my family, my religion — began to lean and tilt.

My father's horrible desires seemed more inflamed by my pubescent body. It was only by going to school and staying out of the house as much as possible that I managed to avoid him. But always there came a moment when he'd catch me at home, and I would be dragged into the cellar.

Once he'd tired of abusing me, he'd order my mother to release me. He couldn't even bear to see me afterward, I suspect because I was a living reminder of his evil ways. He would have been happier if I died, for alive I was a rebuke to him. If he did come face to face with me after abusing me, he'd turn on me — in front of whoever was watching — and slap me.

"She'll never find a husband," he'd jeer, as my sister Sabina watched, "because she's too ugly and stupid! Who'd ever want her? She's not good enough for anyone!" As I stared at the floor in silence, he'd hiss, "That'll teach her a lesson for being so dirty and useless."

My dysfunctional family didn't make the slightest sense to me. The natural love between parents and children wasn't simply non-existent. It was an evil parody. I couldn't for one moment understand how Mum could be complacent. Why did she allow it?

As for Dad, I was starting to admit to myself how much I loathed him. No longer was I living in the hope that he might somehow change, and accept me, and love me as his daughter. I knew that would never happen. And I understood that I didn't need his forgiveness, since the real darkness was entirely his.

I believed less and less in the same things as my family. But at the same time, I didn't have an alternative. At school we were learning about world religions. I knew little about Judaism, Buddhism, or Hinduism, and for the first time I considered properly the many different paths of religious thought and belief systems. Our teacher talked about each religion with the same degree of respect, giving the impression the major faiths of the world were a menu from which we could choose.

Dad considered all religions apart from Islam, as well as atheism, abhorrent. Islam was the one true faith. It was, in fact, his xenophobia and intolerance, screamed at me nearly every day of my life, that made me intrigued by different beliefs and ideas. Writing in my diary each day and thinking to myself on the way to school, I was curious and searching.

In class we learned people convert from one religion to another. This was a revolutionary idea for me. I had assumed one was born into a religion and would remain until death. It was inconceivable that anyone in my community would *convert* out of Islam. Whispered gossip made it clear, the only thing good enough for converts was death.

I began searching for answers to my questions about Islam — questions that I wouldn't have answered until years after. In the school library I saw an English translation of the Qur'an but knew Dad wouldn't allow me to read it. Dad insisted the Qur'an, as rendered in Arabic, was the exact recording of Allah's words. Translation was corruption, and the Qur'an lacked spiritual truth in other languages. The fact that none of us — Dad included — understood Arabic didn't seem to concern him. Dad had learned all of what he assumed to be in the Qur'an at the *madrassa* in Pakistan when he was growing up. He had learned this without questioning his *imam* and from the way people in his village had practiced Islam.

The result was that I — like everyone on my street — had little idea what the scriptures actually said. All we knew were the teachings of Dad and a handful of other religious leaders. None of us questioned this teaching at the time.

At school, my religion teacher began showing me

other religious texts I could read: the Bible in English, the Eightfold Path of Buddhism, the Bhagavad Gita of Hinduism, and the Torah of Judaism. After all my years of Qur'an study, I was finally reading religious texts that made sense. *They spoke to me.* Some of the specific teachings did, too. I loved the story of the Good Samaritan. The contrast with my own faith could not have been more pronounced.

I found myself interested in what these other religions had to say about the relationship believers had with God. In my upbringing, Islam was about submission — blind, painful submission — yet many of these other faiths seemed to be truly enlightening. Adherents sought a personal, uplifting relationship with God, one based upon *understanding* God's holy message.

I was full of confusion. Why did we Muslims pray five times a day in Arabic when we didn't understand a word of those prayers? My entire spiritual life felt like a memorized prayer: mumbled and incomprehensible.

※ ※ ※

One day when I was walking home from school, I saw a white man with a knife shouting wildly in the garden of a white woman who lived on our street. In panic, I called the police. Their arrival to restore peace earned me angry abuse from my parents.

"How dare you call the *goray* police!" Dad ranted. "Why are you interfering? She isn't one of us — can't you leave well enough alone?"

The woman might live on our street, but she was white and English and that made her an outsider. If someone attacked her with a knife, that was *goray* business. The man wasn't a danger to us Pakistani Muslims.

The mores of my community — where a stabbing victim might be ignored because she was not one of us — seemed incredible. What sort of people behaved like this? In my mind, my community and my religion were inextricably linked, and the lessons I drew from this event about Islam were damning.

For the first time, I seriously considered running away. Being abused and treated as the family slave in a dysfunctional home were taking their heavy toll, and I couldn't see sticking around for the sake of my community and my religion. But where could I run? Outside my family and street, I didn't have one single relative or friend who could offer me sanctuary.

There was this, too: if I ran away and was caught, the consequences would be unthinkable. Beyond what my father would inevitably do to me, I knew what happened to girls in our community who tested the boundaries. They were sent "back" to Pakistan and forced into marriage. From there, they never returned.

So, I began to consider suicide. Although Dad hadn't beat Mum for years, she still suffered from chronic headaches that worsened whenever he abused me. To cope, Mum took heaps of over-the-counter pain medication. There were always packets in a kitchen drawer, and we were allowed to take them if we had headaches as well.

I rescued a small pillbox from the trash and began keeping painkillers in it. One by careful one, I took pills from the family stash, certain Mum wouldn't notice. Gradually, I built up a sufficient stock of the small white tablets to kill myself. I hid the box among my clothes, on my shelf in the wardrobe.

I hadn't resolved to kill myself, but I was getting closer. I had no way out. If I reached a point where I couldn't go on, I knew where my pills were. They were the promise of final release from my father.

I was almost fourteen. If I had been told I was being married off in Pakistan, there is no doubt in my mind I would have swallowed every pill. They were my insurance policy, my dark and desperate relief.

❋ ❋ ❋

I was continually aware that I was trapped between two worlds. I didn't fit with my own culture because I was drawn to that of my English friends. But I didn't fit into their culture either, because I was a brown-skinned Pakistani Muslim. I was far from happy with my Pakistani Muslim identity—in fact, I was starting to actively dislike it. But what was the alternative?

It didn't help that I was always dressed in a *shalwar kamiz*. Each month at school there were non-uniform days when the girls showed off the newest fashions, which at the time were "shell" suits—garish, shiny nylon tracksuits. Girls used to wear them with huge hoop earrings, their hair done up in ponytails, and their makeup applied with spatulas. All I ever had to wear was my *shalwar kamiz* and headscarf, in bright canary yellow with no makeup or jewelry. I was mortified.

My friends pretended not to notice my outfit on these days, but others weren't so kind. I was a shy girl, and having people yell *"Paki!"* at me in the corridors didn't help. All I wanted to do was fit in.

I longed for a shell suit. I dreamed of wearing a shiny turquoise one, with bright pink lipstick and blue eye shadow. I just knew I would look great dressed like that.

With Skip gone, I spent most of my time with Sonia, a petite and pretty girl with long black hair and wide brown eyes in the same class as my sister, Sabina. Even at the age of eleven, Sonia had a rebellious spirit that drew us together.

Sonia's house was a terraced Victorian, located between our street and the school bus stop. Her parents were from India and had been living in Britain for about as long as mine. Unlike my parents, however, they both spoke excellent English and worked in the wider community — her father in an office and her mother as a nurse. Sonia's grandmother had been a medical doctor in India, and her family expected women to be educated and independent.

Sonia's life was much freer than mine. She was allowed to go downtown to meet her friends. She was always dressed in Western clothes. Yet she did endure verbal abuse from her Mum, who was always going on about how Sonia's nose was too big — there was even talk of plastic surgery.

Sonia talked to me about her problems, about how she was beginning to believe that her nose made her ugly. I tried to be sympathetic, but from my perspective she had nothing to complain about. In return, I talked to her about how I hated wearing *shalwar kamiz*, and how I was banned from meeting my friends downtown.

But I kept the real darkness hidden. I couldn't bring myself to talk about the way Dad had been beating and abusing me for the last eight years. At some level I felt guilty and ashamed of what was happening, and there was no way I could share that shame with anyone. Since I feared losing a lovely friend — if she discovered how dirty and sick my home life was — I stuck to complaining about clothes.

"Well, there's an easy way around that," Sonia declared with a mischievous grin. "Tomorrow's a non-uniform day, isn't it? Come to my house on the way to school. My parents leave early for work. You and I are about the same size, so you can wear my clothes. We can dress up together!"

I was thrilled. Without considering the risk, I left my house fifteen minutes early the next day and hurried over to Sonia's place. She opened the door and pulled me in.

Upstairs, Sonia had her own room. It was neat and tidy compared to the crowded bedroom I used, and decorated with posters from bands and television shows we both adored. We rifled through her clothes to find me an outfit, quickly choosing a pair of tight jeans and a plain T-shirt. As I dressed, I felt a delicious frisson of excitement. This was the first time in my life I'd ever worn a pair of trousers and felt denim touch my skin!

I stuffed my *shalwar kamiz* and *hijab* into my school bag. Before leaving, there was just time to do our makeup —eyeliner, mascara, and a smear of red lipstick. Mum had made me up once or twice for weddings at the mosque, so I had some idea of what to do. Sonia showed me the rest. Then she did my hair. We looked in the mirror above her dressing table, and decided that we were stunning!

On the front porch, I felt a momentary shudder of terror. "Sonia, what if someone sees me?" I hissed.

She smiled at me. "Come on! You look great. And no one will notice .... Anyway, we've got to go now or we'll be late for school!"

I was certain someone from the community would spot me, and I was right. At the bus stop, I suddenly noticed Amina and Ruhama, two of the girls from my street. They did a double take.

"Wow! Hannan, is that you?" Amina asked.

"Where d'you get those clothes?" Ruhama added.

"None of your business," I replied sharply, with a hint of a threat in my voice.

I didn't want anyone making a fuss—I knew how fast gossip spread on East Street. The fact that I had gone to school wearing makeup and no *hijab* would spread like wildfire. But I was determined to feel normal for just one day, whatever might happen afterward, and I hoped Amina and Ruhama, who were allowed to dress in Western clothes, would keep their lips sealed.

We reached the school gates, and for the first time in my life I wasn't embarrassed at what I was wearing. I had *chosen* to dress like this. The feeling was joy doing a cartwheel in a field of flowers.

Of course, there was one person who made nasty comments—my younger sister, Sabina. "Why are you dressed like that?" she demanded in Punjabi. Her face was twisted into a sneer. "Where did you get that stuff— that *gori stuff*?"

"It's Sonia's," I replied, deliberately speaking in English. "Got a problem?"

"She's a *Hindu*," said Sabina, turning up her nose. "Why are you wearing a Hindu's stuff?"

"What does it matter?" I retorted. "I like these clothes, and I'm going to carry on wearing them."

I was gambling that Sabina wouldn't risk spilling the beans on me at home. If she did, I would tell all her school friends she was a snitch. At home, Sabina was a snitch by nature, but no one liked snitches at school.

At last I felt like one of the girls.

After school the coast was clear. Sonia and I took the bus home and walked back to her house, where I did my transformation in reverse. Off came the jeans and the T-shirt, off came the makeup. My hair went back into a braid. I put the yellow *shalwar* suit back on and replaced the *hijab* on my head. I arrived back on my street dressed exactly as I had left it.

This was the most delicious rebellion that I'd yet experienced; from then on, whenever it was non-uniform day, I dressed at Sonia's house. She was my partner in crime. I didn't want to consider what my parents would do if they found out. Dad's anger would be boundless. But I was willing to take that risk. The reward was a simple, blissful sense of freedom, and that was priceless to me. Everything else in my life — who and how I worshiped, what I wore, what I did with my time, and even my own body — was controlled by my family.

At long last I had done something by my choice, and the taste left me wanting more.

CHAPTER 11

The Outsider

✳

When I was fourteen Raz walked back into our lives. He had been gone for over three years, and there had been no warning he was coming home. Mum hugged him and Raz burst into tears. I was shocked by Raz's appearance and how troubled he seemed.

Raz was a completely different person after his years in the Pakistani *madrassa*. His face had aged and he was painfully thin. Worst of all, his confidence and joy in life seemed to have died. It was like the light in his eyes had burned out, replaced by a vacant, empty darkness.

Raz didn't speak a word to me about what had happened.

One day we heard about a friend of Raz's who was scheduled to go to a Pakistani *madrassa* soon.

"He mustn't go!" Raz blurted out. "Don't let him go. He'll hate it there. It'll kill him!"

Mum didn't know what to say.

"Why? Why will he hate it?" I ventured. "What's so bad about it, Raz?"

Raz looked at the floor. "It's bad because they beat you up," he murmured. "It's bad because they beat you if you get it wrong. And they don't just hit you with a stick, like in the mosque. They smash you to the floor, and you are punched and kicked for hours on end. It's torture. That's what they do. They torture you ..."

I listened in growing horror. "One day, I failed to get the pronunciation of one of the *surahs* right. I kept trying, but I just couldn't do it perfectly. So they beat me and locked me in a horrible, dark room for days on end. *You'll stay in there until you learn to do it properly, and you'll die in there if you don't.* And there were other things too ..."

Raz's voice trailed off into haunted silence; he was afraid to say more.

"I never, ever want to go back there," Raz said, at last. "If anyone tries to send me back, I'll kill myself first."

The brother I knew and loved had been broken down and torn apart, replaced with a wounded young man driven by fear. Later in life, Raz would suffer serious psychological problems, and the *madrassa's* scars would never fade entirely. My father had managed to remake Raz in his own image.

What happened to Raz is all too common. Many *madrassas* in Pakistan prepare boys to fight a *jihad* against the West. They take the boys from their families at a vulnerable age, torture them, and break their spirit. When the boys are under control, they are indoctrinated with hatred and sent off as cannon fodder. Raz escaped that violent fate, but he had been forced to march down a lonely, brutal road.

※ ※ ※

At the top of our street the council of Bermford had built a new school for people with learning disabilities and the long-term unemployed. Many in our community resented that the disabled and "dolies," folks living on government money, were coming onto our street. Most of the adults saw them as the lowest of the low in English society and avoided contact whenever possible.

For many in my parents' generation, a child with a disability was cursed by Allah, punishing you for parental sin. It was a shame on the entire family. In the rural areas of Pakistan, children born with disabilities were often killed or, if they lived, hidden inside the house, perhaps for their entire lives.

Skip's oldest sister, Zaria, had a disabled daughter. Her limbs were weak and she was unable to support herself. If there was a gathering at their house, Zaria's family would hide the little girl away in one of the bedrooms. They loved their little girl, but they couldn't escape the constraints of religion and tradition. Sometimes Skip and I played with her, and the time we spent together taught me that my community's view of people with disabilities was wrong.

On days the school was in session, there was a sense of tension in the neighborhood as the disabled and the dolies arrived. This was the height of hypocrisy, of course—plenty of people on our street, my father included, lived on government benefits. But there was always a difference between them and us.

In my father's case, his status as the *Imam* made his actions admirable by definition. Claiming that his weak back rendered him permanently unable to work, Dad continued to collect government money, even as he officiated at the mosque on a daily basis. He could have learned to speak English, or learned to drive and become a taxi driver. But as far as Dad was concerned, he deserved everything the *gorays* would give him. He didn't seem to feel the slightest bit of guilt that his entire eight-person family survived on benefits. He saw no moral dilemma in taking money from a state he despised, in order to be the spiritual guide of his community.

The dolies were *nothing* like dad, of course. They were degenerates. They wore ripped jeans and leather jackets, and between classes they stood outside the school smoking and drinking. Billy and Zakir might have secretly thought the dolies looked cool, but my brothers had a strong work ethic and wanted to work hard and get ahead.

Most of the time the dolies ignored us. I felt scared walking past them, especially if they'd been drinking, but they didn't shout insults at us or abuse us physically.

When the fighting began in the Gulf War, however, all that began to change. Life became very difficult for us on the street. Whenever we walked past they would yell out: "*Paki*! Saddam-lover! Bloody *Paki*!"

The fact that our families hailed from Pakistan, a part of Asia, and that we weren't Iraqi Arabs seemed lost on them. We were brown-skinned and Muslim, and that was enough.

One day I was walking past with my eldest brother, Zakir, when a group of skinheads turned their hatred and bile on us with full force.

"*Paki* bastards! Little *Paki* bastards! Why don't you f—off home!"

"Shut up!" Zakir yelled back at them angrily. "Shut up! This is my home!"

One of the skinheads leapt off the brick wall where he'd been lounging, ran at Zakir, and punched him. An instant later, the whole gang was on him like a pack of dogs. They hit and kicked my brother, screaming as they did so.

"Get him!"

"Get the *Paki* bastard!"

"Kick his *Paki* head in!"

For a second Zakir tried to fight back, and then he went down under a flurry of blows. He lay on the ground curled into a ball, trying desperately to protect his head with his arms. I screamed over and over as the pack of skinheads kept kicking him. Luckily, Uncle Kramat's son, Ahmed, heard me, and he raced to Zakir's aid. As more of the men on the street mobilized themselves, the skinheads saw the way things were going and fled.

Zakir writhed on the ground in pain. I was terrified. How badly was he hurt? Blood poured from his nose.

Slowly and carefully we helped pull Zakir to his feet, and he told us his ribs were in agony where the skinheads' heavy boots had pounded.

"You okay?" Ahmed asked. "You want me to drive you to the hospital?"

"I'm fine," replied Zakir, spitting out more blood. "No fuss. I don't want any fuss. I just want to go home. Mum can clean me up."

Zakir's nose looked broken and his lips were split and bleeding. He had the beginnings of a black eye. Mum was horrified at what the *goray* lowlifes had done to him. After bathing Zakir's wounds, she told the Pakistani police officer next door, who got the police to come ask a few questions at the school. But nothing more was done. And no one on our street really wanted anything done, either.

Everyone just wanted the whole thing to go away. If anyone was arrested and tried, it would only serve to shine an unwelcome light into our community. We kept to ourselves — that was the way on East Street. From that point, no one ever walked past the school alone. The skinheads realized the whole community was on the lookout, and they never did anything more than call names.

The attack didn't make me feel differently about white people. Most of my friends at school were white, and they stuck up for me. But it did make me feel differently about skinheads. I decided that the skinhead tribe was quite a bit like mine: motivated by blind prejudice and ignorance.

At school older boys who didn't know me began to call me "*Paki*" and "Saddam Lover." Luckily for me, Lara was my champion and none of the boys wanted to offend the most beautiful girl in our year. "Leave her alone, you idiot!" she'd say, her eyes blazing furiously. "She's nothing to do with it! Duh — Pakistan, Iraq. Get the difference? Before you say something even more stupid, best shut up, don't you reckon?"

My community of Pakistani Muslims were mostly anti-Saddam because he was a secular leader who didn't employ *sharia* law (Islamic law) and other Islamic customs in Iraq. At the same time, men like my father didn't like the fact that British soldiers were going to war in a Muslim country. "Look at them!" Dad would declare angrily when there were news reports on television. "*Goray* marching all over Muslim soil. They are taking over the Muslim lands!"

The fact that no Muslim countries were willing or able to go to war on behalf of the Kuwaitis was lost on my father.

❋ ❋ ❋

In Mrs. Zorba's English class I was assigned a book review to present to the class. I chose *To Kill a Mockingbird* by Harper Lee, a novel that tells the story of a white family in the American South, whose father, Atticus Finch, has to defend a black man falsely accused of raping a white girl. To me it was a passionate cry for tolerance, and the need to live and let live—the sort of message my father and the skinheads had clearly never heard.

When it came time to present my book review, I felt sick with nerves. Standing in front of the class, something snapped, and I ran into the girls' bathroom where I cried my eyes out. I felt like a total failure.

At the start of her next lesson Mrs. Zorba stood up in front of the class and announced she was going to read an example of an excellent book review, so the class would have a model to follow. The color rose to my face as I listened to my words being read, but thankfully Mrs. Zorba didn't say it was my essay.

At home, no one had ever said I was good at anything, but at school I was being recognized for my abilities. That year I won the Bermford Comp prize for English. None of my brothers had ever won a school prize before. I read Mum the letter, feeling as proud as I ever had, and she seemed pleased. Dad ignored it, of course, but at least he didn't use it as an excuse to abuse me.

By this time, Zakir and Billy were both away at university. The school award ceremony was to be held in the evening, and neither of my parents wanted to go. Since I wasn't able to go out at night on my own, it looked like I would miss it. Thankfully, Raz offered to act as my chaperone at the ceremony.

"You know," Raz remarked, as he walked me to school that evening, "you've done really well. You should feel good about yourself. This is your big day."

I wanted to hug Raz, and tell him how grateful I was that he'd agreed to take me. But no one ever showed any sign of affection in our household. The only physical contact I ever had was the obscene panting and pawing from my father in the cellar.

My prize included a check for twenty-nine pounds, which was to be used for books. I chose a Compact Oxford English Dictionary, the most expensive book in the shop. Our mayor presented my prize and dictionary to me in front of the local news cameras, and I could scarcely believe what was happening to me.

The dictionary was the first book I ever owned apart from the Qur'an. It was utterly precious to me. I laid it reverently in my hiding place on top of the wardrobe, hoping against hope no one would find it.

CHAPTER 12

The Truant

❀

Unfortunately, my English prize was a solitary bright moment in what was becoming an increasingly dark school record. From the time I first wore Sonia's clothes, my rebellion grew and grew, manifesting itself in increasingly erratic and troublesome behavior at school.

One day we were in a classroom with a storage closet on one side. When our new teacher went inside for some supplies, quick as a flash I jumped up, slammed the door, and locked it from the outside.

For a second everyone stared at me in amazement, and then they burst out laughing. I had always been such a quiet student. *Wow! What a trick Hannan's pulled! Never knew she had it in her!*

I could hear the teacher shouting and banging on the door. I couldn't believe what I had done. As time ticked away, the teacher grew more and more panicked. Just as the class ended, I unlocked the door, running out with everyone else in a swarm that hid my guilt. I knew no one would ever snitch, but I was eventually caught and put in detention where I was made to write 500 times: *I will never lock my teacher in the closet again.*

Mrs. Zorba came to have a talk with me. "I hear you locked your new teacher in the closet. That's not like you. What's going on?"

I didn't really know what to say, so I just shrugged. Even I didn't understand why I had done it. I was rebelling in any way I could, but I wasn't consciously aware of that. I had so few opportunities to break the straightjacket of my life at home, I seized upon any chance at school.

I started to play truant. There was an alleyway a couple of streets away from the school where we girls could sit and chat. There were rarely any boys to flirt with, but there were alcohol and cigarettes to be had. A shopkeeper around the corner was quite happy to sell truants cheap bottles of cider and single cigarettes at ten pence apiece.

I took a drag on a cigarette and tried drinking cider, and neither appealed to me on their own merits. But smoking and drinking were *haram* in my culture, and I was excited by the power I possessed to defy my parents. Because my parents couldn't read or write English, I knew I'd never be in serious trouble for truanting— I could always write my own excuse notes, or prevent them from finding out about my behavior.

Increasingly, however, my problem wasn't how to leave school, but how to escape home. I was growing ever more troubled by my never-ending domestic chores and the dread of what Dad might do to me if I did any-thing to provoke him. While my friends wanted to ditch school to spend more time at home, I wanted to avoid home at all costs.

Sometimes, I was so fearful of going home I would sit in class at the end of school, refusing to go. I did this especially in Mrs. Zorba's class, because I felt I could trust her. Mrs. Zorba would be packing her bag or wip-ing off the blackboard, and she'd glance up to find me alone at my desk.

"Hannan, you're still here?" she'd comment. "No home to go to this evening?"

"There's a *home* all right," I'd mutter. "I just don't want to go there."

"Why not?" she'd ask me gently.

"It's horrible at home," I'd mutter. "I hate it there."

Mrs. Zorba tried to get me to explain. Eventually, I'd admit to her a small part of the reason. "I'm like the family servant. I have to do all the cooking, the cleaning, the laundry—I'm just so tired and fed up with it all."

At times I broke down in tears as I talked to Mrs. Zorba. She was very sympathetic. She would pass me a handkerchief to dry my eyes. But while she tried to help, she had little idea of what my life was truly like. She used to suggest I try sitting down with my mum and dad and having a chat with them about what was wrong. It was all I could do not to tell her how naive and misguided her advice was. Any attempt at a frank discussion with my parents would just earn me another savage assault.

I told Mrs. Zorba I'd give her advice a try, but it was a lie. The more erratically I behaved and the more I played truant, the more concerned she became. Finally, she realized something had to be seriously wrong at home.

"Hannan, I'm really worried about you," she said at last. "Something's really not right at home, is it? That's why you don't want to leave. Come on, why don't you tell me. I can't help you unless I know what's really the matter, can I?"

I started to cry. There was no way in the world I could find it in myself to confess the abuse. What would she think of me if I did? She would be disgusted and appalled. My favorite teacher would surely want nothing more to do with dirty little me.

"My dad's not nice to me," I sobbed. "Sometimes he hits me."

"I'm so sorry, Hannan, I'm so sorry," Mrs. Zorba comforted me. "No parent should ever hurt a child. Is there anything else?"

I didn't say another word. I just cried and cried.

"Look, Hannan, I want to talk to the deputy head about my concerns," Mrs. Zorba ventured. "Is that okay with you?"

"No, it's not okay. Please don't tell anyone. *Please.*"

I didn't want Mrs. Zorba saying anything to anyone, because I didn't want Dad to find out. If he had the slightest inkling I might be spilling the beans on him, my punishment would be unimaginable. As far as I was concerned, my father was all-powerful. How could I ever stand up to him?

Mrs. Zorba gave a sigh. "Hannan, I'm really sorry, but I'm not allowed to keep this quiet. It's my duty as your teacher to report something like this. If a pupil is this upset, it's a sign that she really does need help. I have to say something, especially if I think there might be a danger to you or others in your family."

I'm sure Mrs. Zorba suspected there was more going on than just the physical violence. The signs were there. She hoped I might open up further to a social worker, but the prospect terrified me.

"I can't talk to anyone else, Mrs. Zorba! I'll get into trouble if I do. I just want to talk to you."

"Hannan, listen — you won't get into trouble. So don't worry. These people are professionals, and it is your right to talk if you want to. They talk to teenagers all the time. They're used to keeping secrets. They are here to help. It'll be okay."

With Mrs. Zorba's words calming me, I agreed to talk to someone. A week later, I waited for my interview outside the deputy head's office, almost physically sick with worry. But there was a part of me that really wanted to talk to someone. I was desperate for a way out. Perhaps I could finally unburden myself of all the dirt, guilt, and shame?

I was led into the consultation room.

"Hannan, this is your social worker," he announced,

pointing me in the direction of the lone figure standing by the window. "His name is Omer."

I felt like I'd been punched in the stomach. I grabbed the desk to steady myself as my vision narrowed to a dark tunnel. *Surely they couldn't have . . . .* But they had. Omer, my social worker and my supposed savior, was a Pakistani Muslim. I didn't recognize him personally, but I didn't need to. He was one of us.

Omer was dressed in jeans and a denim shirt. He was tall, with a stubbly chin, and he looked to be in his early thirties. He appeared to be westernized. As I struggled to breathe, he tried a smile. "Hi. It's Hannan, isn't it? I'm Omer. I've come over from the South Bermford office to have a chat with you, okay?"

South Bermford. It was too close. Without a doubt Omer would know my father. I panicked. What should I do? Should I blurt out that it was all a big mistake? *There's nothing wrong at home. The teacher got it wrong. My home life is a joy!*

Not for even one moment had I considered they might send a fellow Pakistani Muslim to speak with me. Perhaps they thought someone from the same religion and culture as me might make me feel more comfortable. In fact, no social worker could have scared me more. I wondered if my father might kill me this time.

I became aware of Omer staring at me, oddly.

"Hannan? Hannan?" he prompted. "Did you hear what I just said?"

I shook my head. "No. Sorry. What?" I mumbled.

"I asked if you're feeling all right," Omer repeated. "You look terrible, white as a sheet. I'm not a scary ghost. I'm just a social worker. There's nothing to be scared of."

There's *everything* to be scared of, I thought.

"Your teachers said you've been having some trouble at home," Omer prompted. That smile again. "What kind of problems are they, Hannan?"

Omer tried to coax me into talking. He smiled so much and was so reassuring, eventually I began to relax a little. He asked me lots of questions and seemed so sympathetic. Perhaps I was wrong to have judged him so harshly, I thought. There were many good people in our community. Perhaps I could talk to him in safety.

Omer asked me why I didn't want to go home at the end of the school day. I told him my family made me do all the housework, as if I was a slave. I said I hated my life and my home. He asked me what I was scared of and why it was so hateful. I told him that my father was ultra-strict and conservative, and I confessed I was scared I would be sent back to Pakistan and forced into a marriage.

I suspected I was being lined up to marry my first cousin on Mum's side. Recently, I'd been shown a photo of him. He was a peasant farmer from the village back in Pakistan. Mum had cracked a joke that they'd decided I was going to marry him. I'd thought, *You may be joking now, but it's probably true.* Mum had gone on and on about what a handsome man he was, and what a perfect match we'd make. I barely glanced at the photo.

In our community, girls were supposed to be married off at the earliest possible age, before they were tempted into dishonoring the family by falling in love. The very idea of marrying for love was the zenith of dishonor, because it proved there must have been inappropriate relations. If a girl was in love, she must have spent time with the man before marriage. The honorable way was to have no contact with the groom prior to the wedding.

In our community, parents were so keen to get their daughters married, they paid a dowry to the groom. Often, the man would get a chunk of money, a teenage virgin British bride, and a ticket to the United Kingdom. He would live with the bride and her family while he learned English and tried to get a job. Normally, he would be illiterate and practically unemployable, fit only for manual labor. Yet this was seen by the parents as a good match, done for the sake of honor.

Omer continued to press me for details. "But why are you so frightened, Hannan? Your teacher tells me you're scared to go home. Is there something you're not telling me?"

"He ... he hits me," I mumbled.

"Your father? Your father's violent toward you? And that's how he forces you into doing things you don't want — like an arranged marriage? Is that it?"

I nodded. "Yes. Pretty much."

I didn't go into any more detail. We were running out of time, anyway. Omer had an hour for me, and it was all but exhausted.

"I'll come back next week, Hannan, so we can continue our chat," Omer assured me. "We can talk as much or as little as you like. So don't worry, okay?"

I didn't know how to feel. That afternoon I walked home lost in thought. Omer had seemed like a nice man after all. Perhaps I would agree to see him again. I went into the kitchen. Mum told me to make some tea and coffee with biscuits and take it to the front lounge for Dad and his visitor.

My mind elsewhere, I knocked and entered the lounge. There, sitting on the sofa next to Dad, was Omer. He smiled at me.

I felt my blood run cold. As I put the tray down, my hands were shaking. I backed out of the room, stumbling over a rough edge of the carpet, and rushed upstairs in total panic. Should I run away? Should I take my pills and end things before my father found me?

Perhaps I was overreacting. Perhaps Omer was still on my side. Perhaps he was just having a good sniff around, checking out my father. Perhaps his visit might even be good for me. There was always a chance.

I didn't have long to think. My father called me and I came down, my legs shaking in fear. Dad was standing in the lounge, his expression like a long-suffering saint with a wayward daughter to help. Instantly I knew that Omer had told Dad everything, and that Dad was doing his best holy man act.

Either Omer believed him, or he didn't give a damn about me.

"Hannan, I've told your father what you said," Omer announced. "He says there's no truth to it. He's assured me he will discuss with you openly your options for marriage. And he's told me he would never dream of striking any of his daughters."

I could hardly breathe. Omer and my father, two Muslim Pakistanis, had reached an understanding.

Omer turned to my father. "As far as I'm concerned, that's the end of the matter. I'm sorry to have troubled you, sir. I'm sure she's a good girl at heart."

It was all so transparent. Omer shook hands with my father, turned and smiled at me, and Dad showed him to the door.

When Dad came back he simply went berserk.

He punched me in the chest, and then he did it again. The second blow knocked me to the ground. There, in the front lounge, he rained down savage kicks and punches all over my body. I curled into a ball, trying to protect myself. Mum was in the kitchen, but I knew she would do nothing to intervene.

"If you ever, *ever* breathe a word to anyone else, I'll *kill* you!" hissed my father, his face swelling with rage. "I'll kill you, and I'll enjoy doing it. You stupid, stupid, stupid, cursed, worthless, evil girl!"

He grabbed me by my hair and dragged me through the kitchen. He threw open the cellar door and shoved me headlong down the stairs. I landed in an agonized heap on the hard brick floor. I knew what was coming, and I began to beg.

My father ignored my pleas.

When he finally tired of abusing me, my father clambered back up the creaking wooden stairs. There was a momentary flash of brightness from the opening door. It swept the darkened cellar like a searchlight, and then the door slammed shut. I heard the key turn in the lock, and then all was silent. I was drowning in the darkness.

I prayed for the Loneliness Birds to come for me.

Suddenly there was a bright flash of golden sunlight, and an eager fluttering above me. They'd come! My beloved white doves had come to the rescue, to carry me out of the horror and dirt to my bright place of rest: the Lavender Fields.

I regained consciousness sometime later. I was covered in cuts and bruises, and every part of me ached in agony. As always, Dad had been careful not to hit me on the face. Beneath my *shalwar kamiz,* no one would be able to see the blue-yellow bruising that was spreading over my burning skin.

In fact, no one would see me at all for a while. I was locked in the cellar for days on end, even though I was supposed to be at school. Occasionally, Mum would bang on the cellar door with a plate of curry. She'd hand it to me with downcast eyes. Mum was determined to ignore the reality of unspeakable evil lurking at the heart of her family.

As I languished in the cellar, I understood there was no way out. I thought again about overdosing. I didn't blame Mrs. Zorba or the deputy head. I had made my cry for help, and my life had descended even deeper into hell. It was time to shut up and survive. Either that, or take my pills.

❈ ❈ ❈

A week later I was back at school and I saw Omer.

"Hannan!" he called out. "We were supposed to meet. How about it? I've got a free hour this afternoon."

I shook my head, I was so angry with him for betraying me. "No thanks."

"No? Why not? Don't you want to talk some more?"

I looked him in the eye. "No, I don't. And you're a real bastard, that's why."

I could see the shock on his face. "Hey, I was just doing what I thought was right—you know that. It's not right to betray your community—"

"Don't you ever come near me again!" I cut in. "You know what? You're shit at your job. You know that? Total *shit!*"

I turned my back and walked away. For Omer, the honor of the community was always more important than the rights of any individual, even when that individual was a child being raped by the *Imam*.

CHAPTER 13

Dirty Little Me

❁

I was fifteen and my GCSEs, my exams to pass secondary school, were fast approaching. I was becoming ever more desperate. I hated my home life. I was totally alienated from my family, culture, and faith. School days were my only taste of sanity, yet I knew sometime soon my education would come to an abrupt and bitter end.

My father was arranging a marriage for me.

Once I'd done my GCSEs, I'd be shipped off to that cousin in Pakistan. Problem solved. Dad's rebel daughter would be gone. Like many girls on our street, I would simply disappear at the end of school.

Dad knew I would never dare complain about what he had done to me once I was safely locked away in my husband's house in rural Pakistan—or I'd face abuse from my new husband too. I would be silenced forever.

I wasn't doing well at school, and Mum and Dad had already told me I wasn't going to university. Pakistani girls didn't go to university, they said, and I didn't argue. I simply kept quiet and hoped somehow things might change.

At that time there was a story on the news about a British girl who had been taken to Pakistan and forced into a marriage. She managed to get help from the British High Commission and escaped. My school friends were absolutely horrified.

"My God, it's so awful!" said Lara. "How can you get married to someone you don't even know? Someone you don't love? Just imagine it! Yuck! Horrible!"

"I don't have to imagine it," I remarked quietly. "It happened to my friend Skip."

Lara couldn't believe it. "What? Who? Here in town? Or in Pakistan?"

"Here," I said. "She lived on my street. Then they sent her to Pakistan for a so-called holiday and forced her to get married."

"But how could a mum and dad do that to their daughter?" Lara asked. "And why didn't she just tell them to get lost?"

"It's part of our culture," I replied bitterly. "They do it to maintain the family's honor. That's far more important than their daughter being happy."

"Oh my God .... Is that what's going to happen to you? Tell me it's not!"

I shrugged. "Yeah, probably. I don't know, but probably it will. And it probably won't be long now...."

"But you can't!" Lara blurted out. "You can't just go along with it. You've got to do something. Talk to your parents! Tell them you don't want to!"

I sighed. "Look, Lara, you don't understand. There's no point talking to them. It'll only make it worse."

It was inconceivable to Lara and my other white friends. At school they had learned about dowries and arranged marriages, so in theory there was a kind of acceptance. But this was different. This was me.

At school our politically safe lessons had avoided the dark and misogynistic side of forced marriages. It was presented as a cultural and religious practice that, while seeming strange to most British people, should be treated with respect and understanding. The reality — that this was often a shocking and brutal abuse of women — was left unreported.

As far as I was concerned, if two people accepted an arranged marriage, that was fine. But a *forced* marriage was very different. I had heard stories of Pakistani women running away from forced and abusive marriages, but because this was a shame on their husband's honor, they had to go into hiding. If the husband or his family — or even her own family — caught them, she would be killed. A daughter's murder was preferable to dishonor.

I'd seen how Skip had been drawn into this trap, and I knew her escape was miraculous. Since I knew my dad was planning my marriage, I decided to push things to the limit, to provoke a confrontation. I understood this non-chance might be my only chance.

I had become quite relaxed about wearing my friend Sonia's clothes on non-uniform days. One day, I decided to walk down our street in my jeans and T-shirt, with no *hijab* in sight. Many people recognized me—I could see the shock and consternation on their faces. I felt a thrill of rebellion and a shudder of fear.

Unsurprisingly, someone went straight to my father. At home I was confronted by Dad's towering rage. "What were you doing?" he screamed as soon as he saw me. He grabbed me by the hair, twisting it savagely. "*Goray* clothes! Becoming like *them*!"

He started to beat me. "Flesh! Showing your bare flesh! Showing flesh like a *gori* whore!"

By now, Zakir was a grown man, physically strong enough to confront and restrain my father. I knew he was home from college and could hear my father's blows landing on my body. But he chose not to intervene, even when my father dragged me toward the cellar. That time, as always when Dad raped me, he coupled it with violence in order to dress it up as punishment, rather than what it was: the satisfaction of his sick sexual desires. I was locked in the cellar for four days.

When I was released, I didn't appeal to my brothers for help. Over the past year, I had cut myself off more and more from my family. I felt like an alien in my own home, and always in danger. I was haunted by my past, terrified by the present, and fearful of the future. My behavior deteriorated rapidly. At school I was withdrawn and sometimes violent.

My English teacher, Mrs. Zorba, could see the pain and confusion that possessed me. One day she spoke to me about it: "Hannan, I know you're having trouble explaining why you're feeling the way you are. Why don't you try writing an essay for me? Treat it like a normal English assignment. Just write down anything that's bothering you."

I called my essay: "Asian Girls in Britain."

When you are a teenager your parents watch you so closely and you have hardly any freedom. You start hating them, because they make you do horrid things you don't want. They make you do all the housework, even though you can't stand it. They want the traditions to carry on. They don't want to change how they live. You can't talk to them anymore, because they can punish you by taking away what little freedom you have. The only freedom you have is at school, but they can stop you going anytime, even though it is against the law. You despise your brothers, because they have more opportunities than you. You have to wait on them hand and foot, like they're kings. You dread leaving school, because life will come to an end. You will lose all your freedom. The thought of running away goes through your mind each and every day.

Mrs. Zorba gave my essay a top mark. But once she'd read it and realized how troubled I was, she tried again to find a way to help me. She asked if I would see a social worker again, but I told her I'd rather die—which is what I knew would happen, one way or another, if my father found out. That was pretty much the end of the matter; there wasn't much more Mrs. Zorba could do.

As my sixteenth birthday approached, my fears grew stronger. One day, Sabina found a passport application on the table made out in my name. "Dad's going to ship you off to Pakistan," she taunted. "Hope you're looking forward to it! Soon you'll be off to meet your *Paki* lover ..."

I wasn't really surprised. I'd known it was going to happen for a long time. I still had the pills in my room and thinking of them gave me a dark and bitter strength.

Yet forced marriage still hung above my head like an angry fist, waiting to strike.

CHAPTER 14

Shackled Bride

By my sixteenth birthday, I was close to suicidal. I did poorly on my GCSEs and knew Dad would use it as the final excuse to ship me off to Pakistan.

Sure enough, my results were abysmal. My best grade was a B in English. Other than that, I had two C's, and the rest were all D's and below. Still, I applied to a sixth form college to retake the exams without my parents' knowledge. That summer there would be an induction day, and I wanted to see what I might be able to study. With results like mine, the options would be painfully limited; but, even so, I clung to a thread of hope. I asked Mum whether I could take the morning off from housework, and to my surprise she said yes. I don't think she even mentioned it to Dad.

At the induction day, I learned I could retake the exams with a view to taking math, religion, sociology, and business studies at A-level. Of course, I got the shock of my life when in due course Dad actually agreed to me going to the college. Oddly it was as if he didn't really care one way or the other, and I wondered what was going on.

I could scarcely believe it when September came and I started South Bermford Sixth Form College. I had been convinced I would be shackled to my "husband" in Pakistan by that time. Sabina told me she had overheard my parents discussing plans for my marriage, yet they had allowed me to attend college. Was I in the clear for another two years? Or were they simply keeping me pacified while they made final marriage plans?

On my first day at college I met Mrs. Jones, the lecturer who would become my favorite. Mrs. Jones taught religious studies and was in her early forties, tall and willowy, with fashionable sandy hair. In class, Mrs. Jones talked openly about her family and began each lesson with personal stories to illustrate the material.

Mrs. Jones doubled as the school counselor, and one month into the term I decided to see her. I needed to talk to someone about my fear of an impending forced marriage.

"Miss, I'm really scared. I know they're planning to marry me off, and send me to Pakistan. I don't want to go."

"You poor thing," Mrs. Jones comforted me. "I have to say I've heard such things before. I've had other girls come to me. Sadly, this sort of thing isn't news to me at all. Have you talked to your parents about how you feel? Can you?"

"No way," I replied. "Dad's the local *Imam*, and my

family's very closed and strict. Talking won't help. In fact, it'll make it worse."

"Well, I'm always here to talk, if you need me. But perhaps if you study hard and get good grades, your parents might see that you should stay at college. These forced marriages are becoming a real problem, you know. The college is trying to work out how to deal with it. We are listening, Hannan, and are here to help you."

As I sat and talked to Mrs. Jones, I felt relatively safe —something I'd never before experienced. But I couldn't make eye contact with her, or with any other adult. I'd look at the floor or the wall, unwilling to let anyone look into me, for fear of what they'd find.

At the end of our conversation, Mrs. Jones said to me: "I know I shouldn't say this, as you are a Muslim, but God really loves you, you know."

"God loves me!" I laughed. "I'll believe it when I see it."

The God I knew was incapable of loving anyone. He was a cruel, avenging God that laughed at misfortune. He sat in harsh judgment and had already condemned me to hell. So said my father, the *Imam*, who also assured me he was going to Paradise when he died.

If my father was the sort of person I'd find in Paradise, I didn't want to end up there anyway.

❈ ❈ ❈

The days were getting shorter, and life continued as normal at home with me doing all the chores. I went to college each day and worked hard at home in the evening.

The next time I made an appointment to talk with Mrs. Jones, she asked me if I wanted to see a social worker. There was no way I wanted a rerun of the nightmare Omer had forced on me. But eventually she talked me around, on one condition: no Asians.

A few days later I met Barry. He was a white guy in his late thirties, small and stocky with a big moustache. He was dressed in a suit and open-necked shirt. His eyes were gentle, and I instinctively felt I could trust him. His smile was as wide as it was genuine.

Barry never spoke to me about honor, shame, or my family's reputation. He simply asked about my fears and worries. He wanted me to talk about myself, free of any religious or cultural constraints. As we talked several times, the bond of trust between us grew. Eventually, Barry gave me a black and white guarantee of help.

"Hannan, if you ever feel that your parents are going to make you do anything against your will, or if you ever feel in danger, you can tell me and I will help you. I'll sort it out. There are ways in this country to really, really protect you."

These were words I had never dared to dream. But could he deliver on his promise? Barry was an outsider — on East Street, my father wielded near-absolute power. Dad could ship me off to Pakistan, and my family and the community would close ranks beside him. Marrying me off against my will wasn't only what they *expected* to happen; it was what they *approved* of. It was what most parents on my street were planning to do with their own

daughters. If anyone ever came to investigate my disappearance, they would throw up a wall of lies and silence.
Everyone would say that I had gone off willingly and was
happy with my new life in Pakistan.

Barry also talked about how I might increase my
confidence. He asked me to write a list of things others
might like about me and what I liked about myself. He
helped me practice making eye contact with him while
we talked. I discovered I could communicate more effec-
tively when I looked at someone. In class, I watched my
teachers — their facial expressions and their eyes — and
my confidence continued to grow. It was a virtuous
circle.

Perhaps Mrs. Jones was right. If I studied hard and
did well, perhaps my parents would let me go to university. I worked harder than I ever had in my life.

In October, Mrs. Jones suggested that the college
send an ad hoc report to my parents, telling them how
well I was doing. A few days later, I carried home an
envelope smartly emblazoned with the Bermford Sixth
Form College emblem. I had to read it to my parents,
translating it into Punjabi:

*Hannan has been working very hard, and the results of
that hard work are becoming clear. She shows great promise. In recent mathematics and religious studies tests, she
achieved excellent marks and was placed high in the class.
In both cases, she also achieved an A for effort. She is a
pleasure to teach.*

Mum was pleased. "Well done!" she smiled.

I was very proud of myself and wasn't going to allow my father's impending negative comment to affect my mood.

Dad snorted in response. "Oh well. That's that then."

❋ ❋ ❋

Two weeks later I had been upstairs ironing. As I walked past the living-room door, I heard my father speaking on the telephone. Something in his tone made me stop and listen.

"Yes, yes — we'll be flying out the day after tomorrow, arriving in Karachi in the afternoon. You'll be there to meet us, is it? Good. Is everything set for the wedding?"

With my ear pressed against the wooden door, I could hear my heart beating in my head. I was shocked and terrified. I'd convinced myself Sabina was wrong, that there were no secret wedding plans afoot. I had started to believe school might be a way out. As far as I knew I didn't even have a passport. *How could this be happening?*

Knowing how rebellious I was, Dad was lining up the final details of my marriage. Allowing me to go to college had been a total sham, designed to control me until he could ship me off to Pakistan. Once I was in the tribal areas and married to a distant relative, Dad's problem — his unwanted, unworthy eldest daughter — would disappear.

The next day I would be forced onto a flight in the evening, after college finished, and my hated father would be sitting beside me.

I ran upstairs to the bedroom, hyperventilating. Panic made my breathing seem to echo off the walls.

In the morning, I would go to college as usual.

And then I would never come home again.

CHAPTER 15

The Escape

❄

Our phone was in the living room, but there was also a phone jack in our bedroom. Often my brothers took the handset upstairs to talk in private. I waited until Dad left the house, then I crept downstairs and took the phone to my room while everyone else was in the lounge watching television.

I dialed the only person I could think of. "Skip! It's Hannan. It's happening tomorrow night. The wedding! They've already got me a passport and a plane ticket. I'm so scared!"

"Oh my God!" Skip's horror reminded me of my own, the night when she had called me from Pakistan, so far away. But Skip, as always, had a plan of action. "Right, let's think. It's tomorrow night after college, is it?"

"After college — the overnight flight to Karachi."

"Then you've got to leave right now."

"I can't! I'm not allowed out at night. Especially alone. Anyway, where would I go?"

"All right, all right .... Well, then you've got to get

out tomorrow morning, or you'll be trapped. Leave for college and that's it. I'll come and pick you up after college in my car, okay?"

"Okay."

"I'll be waiting for you somewhere near the gates. You know the car, so as soon as you see it, jump in."

Skip was working as a secretary and earned enough to have her own car. She was temporarily living with her parents while she looked for another apartment. It was less shameful for her family to have an unmarried daughter living at home, which is why they'd taken her in again. What that meant for me was that I couldn't stay with her, as her parents would never have dared harbor the *Imam's* runaway.

"Where will I go?" I said.

"I don't know. We'll sort something out. Worse comes to worst, you can sleep in my car. Anything's better than your father taking you to bloody Pakistan!"

I didn't sleep a wink that night. I was gripped by anxiety and dark fear. This was do or die. I *had* to get away. I couldn't afford to make a mistake the next day.

I rose at the normal time. As I made everyone breakfast, it was all I could do not to spill the milk over the table. I packed my school bag, hiding a pair of jeans Sonia had given me beneath some files. Then I walked out of the front door, saying goodbye to my little sister, Aliya, for perhaps the last time. I kept my voice normal, though a wild mixture of emotions was threatening to surge out.

I walked up our street knowing I was never coming back. I couldn't go to any of my friends who lived on the street—their parents would simply call my dad. I didn't know if the college tutors could help me either, but I had to try. And there was always the promise made to me by Barry, the social worker. If there was ever a moment when I needed a promise of help to be kept, now was the time.

I arrived at my first lesson five minutes late. For a moment I stood at the back and stared at the lecturer, Mrs. Smith. She knew about my problems because of what Mrs. Jones had told the college board. Suddenly, before I could stop myself, I was yelling at the top of my voice: "I've run away! I'm never going back! Never! No matter what anyone says!"

The class was full. As everyone turned around to stare at me, I could see the worry on their faces. Normally I was shy and quiet, but now I was nearly hysterical.

Mrs. Smith walked back to me and spoke quietly. "Okay, Hannan, it's okay .... We'll sort everything out. Don't worry. Just calm down." She told the class to occupy themselves for five minutes, and she took me to the principal's office. There was no one there, but she put me in a chair and told me to wait.

"I'll call Mrs. Jones and your social worker," she assured me. "But for now just take it easy. They'll be with you soon, okay?"

A few minutes later Mrs. Jones and Barry arrived. I blurted out all that had happened. "My dad was on the phone last night and I heard him, and it's all arranged for this evening, and they're flying me out to Pakistan for an arranged marriage, and I'm not going, and there's no way I can go home tonight! No way!"

Barry glanced at Mrs. Jones, but he was calm. "Right. Well, first off, don't worry. We'll just have to find you somewhere safe to stay. I'll get on it right away. You have my office number? Right, give me a call once you've finished college, and I'll have it sorted. It's nothing to worry about, okay? You're safe with us."

I didn't know if Barry had the power or resources to do that, but I was convinced he would try. In any case, I knew I wasn't going home. I was scared and alone and didn't want to spend my first night as a runaway sleeping in Skip's car, but I was *not* going home.

I spent the rest of the day worrying about what would happen when I didn't go home and where I would sleep. I was so nervous I couldn't concentrate in my classes and doodled on my notepad instead. Someone in the class dropped their pencil by accident and I jumped; the teacher called my name and I jumped. By the end of the day, I was a nervous wreck and still unsure of what was going to happen.

I sneaked out the college gates, and there was Skip in her little blue car! I rushed over and jumped in, telling her everything that had happened as she drove into the center of town. When we neared Barry's office, I stopped to use a payphone. I was dead scared my family might spot me, and I still had no idea whether or not Barry had found me anywhere to stay—or even if I could really trust him.

As soon as I heard his voice, I knew he'd managed it.

"I've got somewhere," he announced. "Everything's okay. Come and meet me at my office, and I'll take you there right away."

My heart skipped with hope. Skip hugged me and drove me round the corner to Barry's office.

"I've found you somewhere safe," Barry told me as he took me to his car. "It's a short drive away. Come on!"

We set off across town. Soon, I realized that we were going to pass by the end of my street, and for an instant fear flashed before me. For one awful moment I thought Barry was delivering me back into the hands of my abusers. I thought he was going to take me back to my father and tell him I had tried to run away. I thought he was going to be just like Omer, my first social worker, and I was terrified. But a moment later we shot past and continued to the outskirts of town, some twenty minutes' drive away.

We stopped in front of a large, brick house with a lawn in front. Barry knocked on the door. I waited beside him, nearly numb with the stress of my predicament and the total uncertainty of my future. Where was I? And who was going to help me?

When Mrs. Jones opened the door, I nearly collapsed.

"Welcome, Hannan!" she declared, smiling. "I'm so glad you're here. Come on in."

Barry and I were taken into the front lounge. Mrs.

Jones shut her two Jack Russell dogs in the kitchen and gave us tea and biscuits. I held tightly to my school bag, feeling nervous and uncomfortable. For my whole life I had dreamed about running away and escaping my family. Now I was finally doing it. There had been no time to think or process anything. Now, suddenly, the shock was overwhelming.

I tried to concentrate on what Mrs. Jones was saying. "...I've got a spare room, and my husband and I are very happy for you to stay here, if you're happy to. What do you think, Hannan? Would you like to stay with us for a while?"

I smiled weakly. I was drifting into shock and was terrified that my family would find out where I was and come for me. My father seemed more powerful than anyone on my side — Barry, Mrs. Jones, or anyone else. I was convinced he would find me.

It was six o'clock. My flight to Karachi wasn't scheduled until close to midnight. My family probably assumed I was walking home from college with friends, yet here I sat on my teacher's couch outside of town.

"Why don't you give your mum a call?" Barry suggested. It was as if he had read my mind. "You should let her know you're okay. She'll be worried."

"No," I answered, fearfully. "Don't let them find out where I am!"

"They won't find out," said Mrs. Jones, gently. "Not from just a phone call. Just tell them you're staying the night with a friend. Don't give them any details. But you do need to call them, so that they don't start looking for you. It's all part of remaining hidden."

I was shown to the phone in Mrs. Jones's hall, and with a shaking hand I dialed home.

As soon as I heard someone pick up, I blurted out: "Hello, I'm okay, but I'm not coming home. I'm staying with friends. Bye."

Before anyone could reply, I slammed down the phone. I didn't even know who it was I had been talking to.

Barry left shortly after, and I sat down to dinner with Mrs. Jones, her husband, and their son, Jonathan. I was amazed at how they went about eating their evening meal. Mrs. Jones and I — the women of the household — sat around the same table as the men, eating and chatting. Her grown son helped set the table. Mrs. Jones served up some strange, gray liquid for dinner, mushroom soup. The only English food I'd ever tasted was chips. The soup wasn't exactly my mother's spicy curry, but Mrs. Jones could have served me broken glass for all I cared.

I had escaped. I was safe. That was all that mattered.

I hardly said a word over dinner. Afterward, Mrs. Jones showed me to a bedroom. It was her adopted daughter Julie's room. There was a single bed, a wardrobe, and a desk for study.

"Make yourself at home," she said. "Julie's away at university, and she won't mind." She paused for a second. "Hannan, would you like to go to college tomorrow, or do you want to stay here?"

I thought about it for a moment. "I'd like to go to college. I'd like to do some study tomorrow, if possible."

"That's great." Mrs. Jones gave me a hug, handed me some folded-up pajamas, and wished me goodnight.

I'd never had pajamas before. At home, we used to sleep in our day clothes. I'd seen them on television, so at least I had an idea what people did with them. Mrs. Jones closed the door, and I was on my own. I was feeling lonely, and unsure of what would happen next. There had been no conversation about how long I might stay.

But in spite of my worries, I was filled with a wonderful sense of relief. Finally, I was away from the threat of abduction and forced marriage. I wouldn't be abused. I felt safe in Mrs. Jones's house — much safer than I had ever felt in my own home.

I cried into my pillow as I drifted into a deep sleep.

CHAPTER 16

Mrs. Jones's House

❋

The next morning breakfast was cornflakes and tea eaten at the table in the kitchen. It felt almost like a dream, eating strange food in a strange house with a *goray* family.

Mrs. Jones's husband was a quiet, gentle man, nearly the opposite of my father. Before sitting down to eat, he smiled at his wife and kissed her. At the table, he commented to Mrs. Jones on what a lovely, charming girl I was. I smiled and blushed. The compliment felt natural coming from him, although no one had ever said such a thing to me before.

Mr. Jones was a lecturer at nearby Leeds University. Jonathan, their son, was in his early twenties and worked as a builder. He was shy, gentle, and quiet, like his father, but he inherited his mother's height and good looks.

On our drive to college, Mrs. Jones told me the story of Julie, the girl whose room I was staying in. Julie was another teenage girl Mrs. Jones had taken in. Over time, she had formally adopted her. She treated Julie as her own daughter, sending her to college and university. Before Julie, Mrs. Jones had rescued a Chinese girl who was in trouble with her family.

If Mrs. Jones told these stories to reassure me, it worked.

We drove right into the college parking lot, and I used the staff entrance at the back. I was terrified that my dad and brothers would be waiting for me, but thankfully there was no sign of them. However, I knew they would turn up sooner or later, and part of me wanted the confrontation to happen sooner rather than later.

Mrs. Jones knew they were going to come too. "Chances are, your family will be here today," she told me, as she escorted me to my first lesson. "But don't worry. We're here for you. You have our total support."

Mid-morning, the principal appeared at the door of my class to have a quiet word with the teacher. I knew instinctively my father had come.

"Hannan, can you go to Mrs. Jones's room?" said the teacher. "The principal will take you there ..."

When we reached Mrs. Jones's office, the principal explained what had happened. "Your father's in my office, and he's demanding to see you. I'm quite happy to send him away, if that's what you want. It's entirely up to you."

I glanced at Mrs. Jones and back to the principal. "Don't send him away," I said. "I want to see him and get it over with. I want him to know I'm not going home. I want him to know he's never going to force me into any marriage. I want him to hear it from me. He needs to know it's my decision, that it's me who's standing up to him."

When we reached his office, the principal opened the door, and I saw my father. He was openly weeping. He was a private man, and his emotional register seemed to include only hatred and lust, yet here he was crying in public, in front of *goray*. For a moment my determination wavered.

And then I understood: It wasn't about me. I could see that his tears were cold and calculated — learning to look adults in the eyes was paying dividends.

"How will I hold my head up high in the community, when you have disgraced us?" my father wailed. "Such shame! Such shame you have brought on us!"

I was beyond all that.

Sixteen years of beatings and rapes had taught me everything I needed to know about my father's supposed shame. As he continued to wail and gesture, I locked onto the remorseless rage in his eyes. I looked into him and understood that he could no longer hurt me, though he wanted to desperately.

"The shame, the shame!" he continued to wail. "Look what you've *done* to us ...." I was no longer listening. I no longer cared.

"No," I answered him, in Punjabi. "I'm not coming home today, and I'm not coming home tomorrow. I'm never coming home."

I turned to the principal. "There's nothing more I

want to say to him. I've told him I'm not going home. My mind's made up."

I left without another word to my father.

Mrs. Jones came with me. "Are you sure you're okay? You were very brave in there."

"I'm fine," I told her. "I'm glad it's over. Can I go back to class now?"

❖ ❖ ❖

That wasn't the end of it. Over the next few days, my father sent every imaginable family member and relative to the college. First came my brothers, one by one, then Mum with my sisters. After that my uncles tried. I refused to see any of them. I left instructions with the college reception that I didn't want to see my family or my relatives. I cut off all communication.

I was too busy adjusting to my new family and my new life to worry about the effect my running away might be having on my father or the community. And anyway, why should I care?

Whenever I did pause to think about it, I didn't relish the fact that they would be burning in shame. I didn't want to hurt my family, or cause them to suffer, but neither did I feel guilty. I was absolutely certain I had done the right thing. I was no longer being abused, and a forced marriage was no longer a looming possibility.

A week into my stay with Mrs. Jones, she took the family to a café for lunch and asked me to go with them. I'd never eaten out, with or without my family. It felt so

odd to have someone I'd never met cook me a meal —
and to pay what seemed like a fortune for the privilege
of eating out. I watched what the others were doing and
tried to blend in.

The Joneses chatted away, lingering over their food.
They asked me to call them by their first names: James,
Felicity, and Johnny. James talked about his week at
work, and the goings on at the Christian church he and
Felicity attended. Felicity (Mrs. Jones) asked Johnny if
he'd like to invite his girlfriend, Zoë, for Sunday lunch.
It was a world away from what I knew.

In my new life, I had so much freedom I didn't know
what to do with it. In the suburbs where the Joneses
lived, no one knew me. I could wander around at will,
unnoticed. I was suddenly free of all the slave-like chores
I had been forced to do at home. I still helped out, of
course, but I wasn't forced to — and I wasn't beaten if I
made a mistake. Freedom, choice, and anonymity were
new burdens I would learn to cope with.

Mrs. Jones encouraged me to stay in touch with my
family, however. I called up one evening and my brother
Raz answered the phone.

"Hi Raz, it's Hannan," I said. "I'm okay. I just want
you all to know I'm okay. I'm staying with friends."

"Where are you?" Raz asked. He sounded worried,
not angry. "Why won't you come home?"

"I'm at a friend's house, Raz. And I'm not coming
home. I'm staying where I am."

"Talk to Mum, will you?" Raz suggested. "She's right here."

"No. I'm going now, Raz. Bye."

I put the phone down. I didn't want to talk to Mum. I knew how she'd guilt-trip me, using tears and emotional blackmail. I knew she'd do all she could to try to get me back. *I'm so ill and it's your fault. I'm sick with worry. I miss you so much. Come home.* It would be hard to hear.

The one link to my old life was Skip, my fellow runaway rebel. I spoke to her on the phone often, and she kept me up to date with the East Street gossip, although I wasn't particularly interested.

"Your parents keep asking me if I know where you are," she'd tell me. "It's a good thing I don't. Let's keep it that way. Then I won't need to lie!"

I wasn't surprised they were trying to track me down. Fortunately, my parents didn't know the Jones's side of town at all. No Asians lived here, so there were no contacts who might report me. I realized they might wait outside the college gates and follow Felicity's car, so we started to keep an eye open for anyone tailing us — especially anyone in a purple Skoda!

A few weeks after my escape, Felicity took me shopping for clothes. The closest I had ever come to shopping on my own was to go to a material shop for the canary yellow *shalwar kamiz* cloth that Mum made me wear. Felicity showed me tops and jumpers and jeans of all colors, and even asked me which ones I liked. I didn't know what to say; I was too embarrassed.

On the way home—the backseat of the car filled with shopping bags—Felicity chatted about Johnny and Zoë. They had been going out for several years, and Felicity hoped they would soon get married. It was all so different from what I was used to, and from the abduction and forced marriage I had so narrowly escaped.

"I'm never, ever going to get married," I remarked quietly.

I meant it, too. After what my father had done to me, the thought of having a physical relationship with any man was just repulsive. I didn't think I could ever trust a man in that way. All I had ever known was dirt and pain and abuse and darkness. I hadn't told Felicity about my father abusing me. I guessed she presumed my anti-marriage sentiment was due to a narrow escape from a forced marriage.

Felicity laughed. "You might change your mind in the future!"

"I wouldn't bet on it," I replied.

"Well, you never know. One day you might meet the man of your dreams and fall in love."

We continued to drive in silence. I stared out the window with a determined look on my face, trying not to think about what Felicity had just said. I could never fall in love with any man; I would never fall in love with any man. Not me!

CHAPTER 17

Apostasy Pending

One Sunday shortly after I ran away, Felicity took the family to church.

"Make yourself at home, Hannan," she said. "We won't be long."

On the spur of the moment, I asked if I could go. It wasn't that I was frightened of being on my own. In fact, I was happy with my own company. But I wanted to see her church.

Felicity hesitated. "You really don't have to come, you know. It's not necessary."

"But I want to go. I want to see what it's like."

Felicity took some convincing. Because she was my religious studies teacher, she was being doubly careful about not influencing me. I had to convince her I wanted to go of my own free will.

Here was this person letting me stay in her house, in spite of the potential risks. I wanted to know more about her and her family—including their belief system. The idea of my parents inviting a fugitive stranger of another race and faith into their home was a total impossibility. Was Mrs. Jones's religion one difference that helped explain such incredible generosity of spirit?

It had been drilled into me that I was a useless, godless child destined for hell, and I believed it. I knew I would never be good enough for my parents' God. When Felicity had told me her God loved me, all those months ago at college, I had scoffed. How could there be a *loving* God? I was intrigued by Felicity's idea of God, even while I didn't believe it could be true.

The church was built of aged, gray stones. It was Methodist, Felicity said, a term that meant nothing to me. Entering by the front steps, I saw row after row of wooden pews already packed tightly with churchgoers.

I was the only non-white person there.

At first I received some odd looks, but once Felicity introduced me, people were friendly. Our chatter died down — something for which I was grateful — when Felicity's husband began to play the piano at the front of the church. As the music flowed and swelled, I gazed at the beautiful stained glass windows and the ornate carved pillars. It struck me that it had a special presence. There was a sense of peace here that I hadn't experienced before, and I was intrigued by it. A hymn was sung. I listened, but I didn't know any of the words. Felicity tried to point them out to me, running her finger along the lines in the hymnbook as she sang. Then there was a reading from the Bible, followed by the sermon.

The pastor was simply referred to as Bob. He was in

his mid-fifties, and I was immediately struck by how human and intimate his sermon seemed. He started off by telling a story about something quite ridiculous that had happened to him over the weekend. I glanced around furtively, amazed as everyone laughed at Bob's mishaps. No one would dare to laugh at a Muslim holy man like my father—and he would never deign to tell such a self-deprecating, human story.

My amazement continued to grow. Bob spoke with laughter and joy, and the excitement in his voice seemed to show his true affection for both his topic and his congregation. When we sang, Bob led from the front on his acoustic guitar—only his repertoire of chords was so small, he was forced to play "air guitar" during measures of each song.

The service closed with one final hymn. As the congregation took up the melody, the words came floating back to me, for I had sung "Amazing Grace" with my junior school choir. I had really loved that hymn as a child, so I self-consciously sang along. I was surprised that people were so joyful here. The volume of the singing went up and almost raised the roof, which made me realize this hymn was a church favorite.

I left feeling happy and intrigued. I was fascinated to know how the pastor could be so relaxed, even to the extent of mocking himself in a public house of God. Bob seemed excited by his faith, and by the life of Jesus in particular. I had been told by my father never to mention Jesus' name in our house—what about him was so compelling to Bob and others?

The following Saturday I asked Felicity if I could go again. That Sunday there was a whole new sermon from Bob, "Amazing Grace" to finish again, and more funny stories in between. There was more excited talk about Jesus, too. For the first time in my life, I found myself enjoying being at a place of worship.

Since the sermons and readings were in English, I could understand everything. The prayers, especially, made sense to me. People prayed for those who were ill, and even for people from other countries and religions who were poor or unfortunate. They prayed for whatever misfortune had happened that week—an earthquake in South America or flooding in Bangladesh. There seemed to be a concern for the wider world, regardless of whether the people in question were Christian or otherwise. Our prayers at the mosque were always set verses from the Qur'an that never seemed to vary.

God is great,
God is great,
There is only one God ...

What surprised me most was that Christians prayed for people of other faiths to be healed and helped. In Islam, we understood the concept of *zakat* (charity) but in my father's interpretation it was always about helping other Muslims, even though I was to learn later that the Qur'an extends *zakat* to all needy and poor people. For my father, charity was only ever extended to the *Ummah*, the global community under Islam. At the mosque we raised money for earthquake victims in Muslim countries, but an earthquake in Peru, for instance, wouldn't merit the slightest concern.

✻ ✻ ✻

The months I stayed with the Joneses were some of the happiest days of my life. I even went on holiday with them. We spent two weeks by the seaside in Cornwall, camping at a place called Coverack, near Lands End. It was the first time I had spent time near the sea, and I began learning to paddle in the waves.

Our campsite had a breathtaking view over the water. Each morning we ate outside, gazing over the vast expanse of ocean rolling out before us. It took my breath away. I found it beautiful and freeing. As a Muslim, I couldn't eat the bacon or sausages Johnny fried up on the portable gas stove, but I could enjoy the mouth-watering smell.

One day after a morning on the beach, we visited the local art gallery, located in a beautiful stone cottage. We wandered around the gallery admiring the seascapes and other works, and followed that with an enormous cream tea at the attached shop.

I felt like I'd woken from a nightmare and entered a sweet dream.

Camped on the cliff tops in the fresh sea breeze, I didn't think much about my old life. I was simply relieved to be out of it. The slavery, the threats, the fear, the isolation, the abuse—I longed for the wind to carry all of that away across the whitecaps. I had not needed the

Loneliness Birds to carry me off to the Lavender Fields since I had left home, but I still ached with the knowledge that my family had not loved me. I was unlovable to them. I wanted to belong, and for the wind to carry away — in that moment and forever — the feeling of dirt and guilt I had when I thought of my father.

* * *

Week after week I sat quietly in my pew, just watching and listening. The care and the love I experienced from the Joneses had to come from somewhere, I reasoned. If it came from their God, perhaps I should try to get to know him. I started attending the church youth group, and it was there I met Rachel.

Rachel was from a typical white northern English family. Her dad was a social worker, and a real gentleman. Her mum was a teaching assistant in a primary school. Rachel was a petite, blonde bombshell. She was two years younger than me and very popular at school.

I found it funny that this petite angel spoke with such a strong northern accent. Mine was still tinged with a Pakistani lilt, but the longer I spent away from East Street the more it faded. I was happy to hear it go. Apart from my skin color — which I could never change, nor did I want to — I was happy to dispense with just about anything that reminded me of my former life.

Rachel helped ease me into the process of being a free young woman. She took me clothes shopping and helped me experiment with makeup and jewelry. We played Scrabble—my favorite when I found I had a wide vocabulary from all those lonely hours spent reading. Sometimes I slept over at Rachel's and we'd talk for hours on end.

Whenever we could afford it, Rachel and I went to the cinema. I had never been to a movie before and was enthralled by *Titanic*. What appealed to me most was the romance—the idea that Leonardo DiCaprio's character would die to save his love. I liked his sense of humor, too, and the fact he was an artist. That sort of love was the kind I would love to find … maybe one day.

As I continued my education and tried to get into a routine of college during the week and weekends spent with Rachel and other friends, I needed to find ways of supporting myself. Felicity suggested I apply for educational grants and Housing Benefit through social services. Felicity dropped me off at the benefits office where I told the supervisor, a young white man, the full story of fleeing my home and a forced marriage. He took me into an inside office where he started to fire questions at me. Finally, he started demanding my family's details.

"You have to give me your parents' phone number," he said. "I can't process anything without that."

"But what do you need it for?" I asked.

"Well, if nothing else, I have to verify your story. I can't just take it at face value, can I?"

"But you don't understand," I protested. "I just told you I've run away from an arranged marriage. I can't risk them knowing where I am, or what I'm doing."

He shrugged. "We can't give you benefits without verification. It's very unlikely we can help you, anyway. Most likely you'll have to go home to live with your parents."

I was getting scared. He kept going in and out of the back office to speak to someone else, then coming back with more questions. He told me point blank, I had to go back to my father's house because my family should be supporting me, not the benefits office. He kept demanding the phone number, so he could call them up and "arrange things."

"There's no way I'm giving you my parents' number," I said. "It's getting late. I have to go."

With that I got up and scurried out of the office. As soon as I was outside, I burst into tears. I went to the nearest phone box and called Felicity.

"Wait right there!" she ordered. "I'm coming over to have words with them!"

She drove straight from college, and we went back inside together.

Felicity asked me which man I had spoken to and marched straight up to him. "How *dare* you tell this young girl she has to go home," she announced. "You know *nothing* about her situation. You don't have a clue, and yet you're telling her she has to go home!"

"And who are you?" the man demanded, rudely.

"I'm her college tutor," Felicity fired back. "And I'm also her guardian. If you persist with this behavior, I will immediately inform the college principal and her social worker. This is totally unacceptable. We may even have to report it to the police. This girl's very life could have been endangered by your actions!"

The man was looking worried now. He could tell that Felicity meant business. "Look, I'm sorry," he said. "I didn't fully appreciate her situation. I was just trying to verify ... "

"Verifying she's telling the truth doesn't require forcing her to return to a dangerous and abusive family, does it?" Felicity countered, icily. "Or am I missing something?"

"Erm .... Look, why don't we start over?" asked the man nervously. "We'll fill in a whole new set of forms, and get the application underway for educational grants and Housing Benefit. Let's just forget I ever said anything about her family, okay?"

By the time we left the office, I was exhausted. Exhausted and exhilarated. For the first time in my life, someone who loved me had stuck up for my rights. My father told me time and time again that all white English people were drunks, and whores, and brawlers; but like so much else it was blind prejudice and lies. There was another England, different from the one depicted by my father. It was an England populated by the Mrs. Joneses of this world — good, honest, open-minded, tolerant people, whose faith gave them courage to confront evil.

I thanked God for Mrs. Jones.

I just wasn't sure whose God I was thanking.

I was confused.

I was a Muslim, and so I believed I would remain all my life. I didn't feel like I was doing anything wrong by going to church. I'd been taken to churches on junior school outings, so it wasn't completely alien to me. But I was confused about who God was. I started to wonder if it was possible for me to become a Christian, and then I could pray to Mrs. Jones' God.

CHAPTER 18

My Church

❄

I spent Christmas with my new family. In my home, Christmas had been no different from any other holiday —except there were better films on television. We were a Muslim family in a Muslim community, so there was no Christmas tree at home, no decorations, and no presents.

I did get the odd Christmas card from school friends, and Mum secretly gave me money with which to buy cards and stamps so I could return the favor. But I hid the cards in my school bag, and once Christmas was over I threw them in the trash so Dad wouldn't find them.

In Felicity's home, we spent all afternoon decorating the Christmas tree, along with the entire house. I breathed in the scent of pine from the freshly bought tree, and we put lots of blue and silver ornaments all around, adding silver tinsel to match. The final touch was the Christmas lights.

Later, we wrapped presents and heaped them beneath the tree like a rainbow avalanche. I savored the electric buzz of anticipation in the air; I'd never felt anything like this at home. The weather outside was wet and miserable, and coming into a festive house to sit in front of an open fire felt perfect.

On Christmas Eve we went to church for midnight service. As people arrived, there was a sense of expectancy in the air, of love being shared, and of Bob telling the Christmas story. I had seen the nativity plays at primary school, but this was the first time I really understood. Bob repeated the phrase "God became man"—which echoed inside my heart. I was amazed that God could become something as humble as a normal man, simply so he could be in relationship with human beings. I had expected God to rant and rave about how bad we humans were, not emphasize the love Bob kept talking about. God's *love* made him come to earth as a man to communicate with us and care for us. Bob stressed the word over and over: Love. Love. *God's love.* I felt my heart racing as Bob spoke, and I wanted to know Jesus. I wanted to be a Christian.

Felicity's adopted daughter, Julie, was sitting next to me on the pew. Eventually, I leaned across and whispered in her ear. "How does someone *become* a Christian?"

Julie smiled. "Easy. You just ask Jesus to come into your life. Ask him to forgive your wrongs, and give thanks that he died on the cross and rose again for you."

"And that's it?"

Julie nodded. "That's it."

"There's no other words you have to say, nothing you have to do in public or anything?"

"No. None. You can get baptized if you like, but you don't *have* to."

This seemed to me to be such a private, personal thing, and I rather liked it being so. In order to become a Muslim, one has to repeat the following phrase three times, in front of an *imam*: "I bear witness that there is no God but God, and that Mohammed is his true prophet." Once that was done, you would be declared a Muslim. I had presumed there would be a similar formality to Christianity, but it seemed in this church there was nothing but this private prayer.

I returned to the Jones house and went to bed, hoping to dream about the piles of presents under the tree. But I couldn't sleep. I kept thinking about Bob's words and what Julie said to me. So I prayed and, for the first time in my life, I prayed to a Christian God: "God, if you are real, if you exist and you are a loving God, then I want to know you, and I want you to come into my heart." I never knew it was possible to have a relationship with God before the moment I prayed this prayer, and it really felt like a two-way communication. I sensed God say, "Yes, I am here. I do exist, and I love you."

In that quiet moment I converted from Islam to Christianity!

The impossible had been made possible. I didn't really think about it like that at the time. I didn't think about the past—the last sixteen years of being a Muslim. I didn't think about the faith of my birth. I was just lost in the emotion of the moment. I didn't even consider what my changing faith might mean. I was ecstatic that there was a God who loved me and wanted a relationship with me. Me! I wanted to shout it to everyone, but I decided to keep it to myself for now and secretly enjoy the start of my new reason for living: my relationship with God.

On Christmas Day we exchanged our presents. I had never unwrapped a present before, so I watched what the others did. I saw them opening their parcels in front of each other, and smiling and saying thank you. I tried to follow suit, but felt awkward as I didn't know how to respond to a family member giving me anything. I didn't know what to do or how to act. But I did know I was happy—happier than I'd ever thought I could be.

I started to read the Bible and found that I wanted to read it all the time. I read Matthew's Gospel, then Mark, Luke, John, and I continued on excited by the stories about Jesus and parables that he told. I read the Psalms, which calmed my fears and helped me sleep at night.

As I read the Bible, I was learning what it meant to be a Christian, about how Jesus would want me to live my life. I was embracing this newfound freedom to be myself, and most of all I was learning I was loved. It wasn't about being worthy or deserving any more. It wasn't about working hard to be accepted. It was about knowing the love of God was there in spite of everything I did wrong. More than anything, I felt an inner peace and sensed a flicker of hope. There was a light in my heart where there had been darkness.

✳ ✳ ✳

I managed to keep my conversion private for a few weeks. One afternoon, while I was eating lunch with the family, I decided to say something. I glanced around the table nervously. "On Christmas Eve ... well, um, I—I think I became a Christian."

A huge smile lit Felicity's face as she jumped up and hugged me. We danced around the living room while each member of the family hugged me in turn—a foreign practice with which I was becoming increasingly comfortable.

One part of me thought the Jones family was a bit crazy, the way they danced and laughed so excitedly. But another part of me liked the uninhibited way they showed their emotions. There was a freedom and a lightness in it that refreshed me.

Felicity understood the significance of my conversion. She knew it could cause me real trouble—life-threatening trouble—and this worried her greatly. I had run away from my family and my culture, and now I had run from my religion, too. But for the moment she was happy to concentrate on being overjoyed for me.

I'm glad she didn't voice her concerns then. She gave me the freedom to make my own way—and to make my own mistakes if necessary. I had been rigidly controlled for too long. No longer would honor and shame dominate my decisions.

I knew once my conversion was known, the Muslim

community would ostracize me. But if that happened, I told myself, those friendships weren't genuine, and never had been. With Felicity, Julie, Rachel, and Zoë, I had seen friendship and love given in spite of danger and risk—and given across a cultural divide.

This was the meaning of true friendship, and I vowed to chase it.

CHAPTER 19

Moving On

❈

Several months later I moved out of Felicity's house. I took a room I had been offered by the Project for Accommodation in Bermford (PAB), a housing association for young people bereft of family support.

Living with Felicity and her family had saved my life, but now I wanted to push the boundaries of my independence and freedom. I wanted to stand on my own two feet for the first time in my life. There were so many things I'd never had to do: manage my own finances, shop and cook for myself, find a job, and manage my own schedule. That's what most people my age did, and I wanted the same.

I stayed in my new PAB accommodation for eighteen months, during which I increasingly focused on my college studies. I knew I absolutely had to perform well. I had turned my back on my family, my religion, and a forced marriage, and now I would have to survive on my wits alone.

I saw Felicity and her family often. Johnny took me

to church most Sundays, and three or four times a week I traveled back from college with Felicity to eat dinner at her house.

Yet even with that support, I began to worry that perhaps my bid for total freedom had been premature. Too much had happened to me too soon, and I was increasingly unable to compartmentalize. Crucially, I was denying the real horror I had been through — the abuse — in an effort to embrace a bright and free future.

It was hardly surprising when I began to fall apart. I became so depressed that I volunteered to enter a mental health ward, even though I wasn't ready yet to reveal the full extent of the abuse I'd suffered.

Who was I? I was a British Asian-born Muslim who had converted to Christianity and befriended a bunch of white Britons. Where on earth did I belong? My friends at church loved me and cared for me, but how could they understand my background? Meanwhile, my family rejected the person I had become.

I didn't regret leaving home or becoming a Christian. Far from it. But I simply had no idea how to live my new life. I was diagnosed with clinical depression and put on anti-depressants. The medication made me feel like sleeping constantly, but still I entertained a steady stream of visitors: Felicity came nearly every day, and Zoë, Johnny, and Rachel often came with her. My tutors and the college principal visited, and even Barry, my social worker, stopped by.

With time, my spirit seemed to heal, and I checked

out of the hospital to get on with my life. I felt like I had just begun a long journey toward telling the full truth of my life. However, I knew the cost would be terrible, and the journey achingly long. I needed the strength to continue.

I spent a lot of time at Felicity's house, gradually building up my energy. One morning we were having breakfast, and Felicity placed bread, fried rashers of bacon, and tomato sauce on the table. Everyone tucked in, and without thinking about it I made myself a bacon sandwich. As soon as I bit into that sandwich, I realized what I had been missing—it was one of the most delicious things I'd ever tasted.

I glanced around, waiting for someone to comment, but no one said a word. I didn't consider the significance of that meal until later. *Oh my goodness, I've eaten pork!* I fully expected to be sick as I waited for something horrid to happen. But nothing did.

After that, I was a fan of bacon. It was one more step away from my family and toward a future that scared and attracted me simultaneously.

Many other things surprised me as well about this new life and the people in the church. For example, I found it shocking when I first saw the people in my church put their Bibles on the floor. In my mind they were disrespecting a holy book, as Muslims would never dream of putting a Qur'an on the floor. I had to get used to so many differences in culture and in religion, and I knew it would take me a while.

❄ ❄ ❄

Whenever I phoned Mum, she'd launch into a guilt-soaked litany of complaints. "You're making me so *ill* like this, you know," she'd whine. "My health's suffering. We all miss you *so much*. When are you going to come home?"

Every time my answer was the same. "Mum, I'm not coming home. You know why I'm not coming home. *You know.* You have to come to terms with it. I do want to stay in touch. But I'm not coming home."

She never once said anything suggesting she cared for me or that she was sorry. I was moving on, but my mother was still blaming me for all her ills. I was still the guilty one—still, in my father's eyes, in need of punishment.

I remained in contact with Skip as well. Her new apartment had become a haven for girls from our community who had been threatened by or forced into abusive marriages. During one visit I met three sisters there who were older than me and several years into their arranged marriages.

Each had been sent to Pakistan to marry a total stranger from a remote village. They had then returned to the UK with their husbands. Five, six, and seven years later, their lives were sheer hell. The sisters lived together in one house with their husbands who worked as manual laborers in nearby factories. Each of the sisters had completed secretarial studies, but their husbands would not allow them to work outside the home.

Of course, they were regularly beaten. They were treated as domestic slaves, waiting on their husbands hand and foot and answering to their every need. Worse still, their husbands often got drunk on cheap alcohol and tried to share the sisters in bed.

The sisters bolted the bedroom doors so the men couldn't come in. They would keep knives under the pillows in case they had to defend themselves. However, they feared they wouldn't be able to fight their men off forever. They couldn't tell their parents what was happening, for it would bring shame on the family—and they felt deeply ashamed about it themselves.

They knew sex without consent was rape, and that rape was illegal in the UK. But how could they go to the police, for nothing would bring more dishonor to the community than that. Turning to the *imam* for help would be worse than pointless—I knew that all too well.

Skip and I were horrified. We realized how lucky we had been to escape our own forced marriages. But what advice could we give them? All we could say was that they should leave their husbands. But they were too afraid to do so: afraid of the shame, the dishonor, the rejection by their families, and of being ostracized by the community.

I knew the sisters wouldn't do anything to get out of their situation. They couldn't bring themselves to risk their lives and the honor of their community. Seeing how frightened, miserable, and trapped they were, I was doubly relieved to have made my own escape.

❀ ❀ ❀

My family had attempted to imprison me in a coffin of shame. I understood my conversion out of Islam to be the final demonstration of my refusal to be so imprisoned. I called Billy and arranged to meet him in a local park. He greeted me with a big smile. I asked him how everyone was.

He shrugged. "You know, same old same old ... Mum's asthma is getting worse. Everyone blames it on you. Ever thought about coming home?"

"I don't want to, Billy. I'm never going to do that. But there's something important I want to tell you. I've become a Christian."

He laughed. "Come on—you can't be serious!"

"I am serious. I've converted."

"It's all part of your rebellion," Billy countered. "I know you're going through a bad patch, but you'll see sense and come home. You're a Muslim, Hannan. A Muslim."

"Billy. You're not listening. I've converted to Christianity. I am a Christian. D'you really think I'd be welcome home now?"

Billy shook his head in despair. "You were born a Muslim, Hannan. You'll always be one. You'll die one, too. This conversion stuff—it's bull."

"I am a Christian, Billy. I've made my choice. And sooner or later you'll have to accept it."

Billy wasn't angry or aggressive. He just thought it

was another chapter in the story of his younger sister's temporary rebellion.

But I knew that old story was over, and now I was writing something new. I was becoming a new person — a person I was starting to like.

CHAPTER 20

Baptism of Blood

A rough hand seized me and shoved me toward a small, horribly familiar wooden door. I tried to scream, but no sound came out. The hand grabbed my hair and jerked my head backward. I could see the fury and the contempt in the eyes. Dragged down the rough brick steps, down into the cold shadows, darkness overwhelmed me. I was back in the hands of my abuser.

I woke with a jolt.

The recurring nightmares were always the same: a flashback to the horrors of being abused in the suffocating cellar.

I was feeling desperate and increasingly alone. I hadn't told anyone that my father had raped me for over a decade. Felicity had become like a surrogate mother to me, and I became increasingly convinced that telling her about my past was the only way to begin healing. One day after lessons, I stayed behind with Felicity at college. I began to talk, and I was able to tell her some of what had happened, before I broke down in tears. I felt

Felicity wrap her arms around me, warm and protective, as she hugged me and held me tight.

"Oh, Hannan, my poor dear. I love you. God loves you. You will get through all this, you will."

I asked her not to tell anyone, but she told me that wasn't an option. She was my tutor and my guardian, and she had a responsibility to report what Dad had done. Knowing the depths of his abusive ways, she was worried for my sisters' safety. I guessed she was right to be fearful. Sometimes I feared for their safety myself, especially now that I was gone.

"I'm afraid of going to the police," I told her. "I don't think I'm ready to tell them. I can't bear the idea of going into the detail they'll need. I just don't want to dig up all those horrible memories, especially with strangers."

I knew what would happen to my family, and the community, if Dad was arrested for sexually assaulting his daughter. An *Imam* being tried in a British court for raping his own child from the age of five to fifteen would tear the community apart.

What was more, I doubted the police would believe me. I was just a young college student, while my father was a pillar of the community. I remembered how Omer, the social worker, had immediately accepted Dad's word over mine. It seemed inconceivable to me that the police would hear me out and believe me. It went against all I had experienced. I explained all of this to Felicity.

"I understand your concerns," she said. "But how

about if we talk to Barry? Maybe he'll know what to do. Would you be willing to do that?"

"Okay," I said. "I'll try."

A day or so later I met up with Barry. He was such a kind, supportive presence, I was able to tell him some of what had gone on over the years. As he wasn't part of the child protection team, he had to refer me to them. A social worker from that team came to speak to me. Her name was Vicky, and she told me I absolutely had to go to the police. I didn't see that I had much choice, so I agreed.

Vicky drove me to the police station, where a female officer took me into one of the interview rooms. We sat at a desk and she set a small tape-recorder running. She had a sheet of paper before her and a pen poised at the ready.

"Right, Hannan, tell me in your own words exactly what happened. Start with your name and where you used to live, and we'll go on from there."

"My name is ... My name is Hannan Shah. I ... I ... I ... "

I tried to get the words out, but I froze. My throat clammed up. I started shaking, and tears welled up in my eyes. I was terrified about what might happen if I went ahead with this. I was terrified for myself. The physical act of forcing myself to talk made me panicky, especially with strangers. And I knew if I went ahead with this statement it would launch a series of events that could never be stopped.

"I ... I ... I can't do this," I managed to stammer. "I just can't."

The police officer was calm. "If you're not ready, just come back when you are, okay? Don't worry. It's not a problem for us. We need you to be comfortable and ready."

That reassurance was crucial for me. I decided I would try to pluck up my courage for another day. Vicky, the child protection officer, said she would take me home. For a while we drove through the streets in silence. Then she gave me a sideways glance.

"Well, Hannan, you really messed up, didn't you? You were completely *useless* in there. You didn't tell them a thing. What a waste of everyone's time!"

I couldn't find the words to reply. I started crying and shaking again. All the way home she berated me for being so useless. Once she'd dropped me off, I called Barry. He was enraged and called Vicky's supervisor to lodge a formal complaint. But the damage was done. I wouldn't be able to go to the child protection officers for a very long time.

In due course the child protection team went to the primary school to check on my little sister, Aliya. If there were any signs of abuse, or if the teachers had any concerns, they would put my sister on the "at risk" register. Thankfully, there was nothing. I was so relieved. I didn't think Dad would be doing the same to her as he had to me. To my knowledge, he had never beaten her, but I was still relieved.

Despite everything, I still cared about Mum, my sisters, and my brothers. Reporting the abuse would be the beginning of the end for them all. It would hurl them into an abyss of torment, shame, and dishonor. As long as I thought my sisters were safe, the cost of going public about Dad was too great for my family. I didn't want them left to live without a husband and a father. However cruel and evil Dad was, in our culture they would have been even worse off without him.

❋ ❋ ❋

One day, Rachel and I went ten-pin bowling with two boys from her youth group. It almost felt like a double date. One of the guys, Ian, was Felicity's nephew. He saw me again at my Bible study class on Sunday evening. After class, he sidled up to me.

"Hi, Hannan," he said, nervously. "Um ... I really like you."

I blushed. What on earth was he saying? I felt so ugly and worthless. My family had always said so. What on earth could this tall, handsome, blue-eyed blond see in me? Maybe he could see the person I was becoming.

"I'm going out with some of my mates on Tuesday," he was saying. "Would you come with me? Like, on a date?"

"I'd like that," I stuttered, still not believing what was happening.

He turned up that Tuesday evening and we walked to the venue—bowling again. As we strolled along the street, he reached out and held my hand. I almost drew it away instinctively. Being close to a man felt so odd to me, and would have been the cause of juicy gossip and scandal on East Street!

But I told myself to relax and savor the moment. I knew it was innocent. We were hardly a match made in heaven, in any case. Ian was obsessed with soccer, and later when I cheered for the wrong team at a match—and he hugged the girl sitting on the other side of him—I was glad to move on. What mattered was that I *could* move on. I could like another boy, or stay single, all in my own growing freedom.

All this time I was studying as hard as I could. When I finally took my A-levels, I earned high marks in sociology, theology, and English. I was ecstatic and immensely proud. I had done well enough to enroll in the social sciences program at Lancaster University. It was a dream come true.

❊ ❊ ❊

Bit by bit my life was getting better. While I was away on a church trip to care for orphans in India, my friend Rachel had found me a lovely place to live. A family from the church had offered to rent me a room in their house. It was good to be living with a family again after my stint of going it alone.

One day I went with Rachel to visit a church where she had some good friends. After the service I spotted an elderly white lady who looked somehow familiar. It suddenly came to me: she was Edith Smith, the woman who had come to our family home to teach Mum English all those years ago. I introduced myself.

She smiled at me. "Yes, I do remember, you know. And your delightful mother, how is she?"

"Well, I don't have too much to do with her," I explained. "Mum's okay, I think. But I've become a Christian, so I have to keep a bit of distance."

"How extraordinary! Well, you must come back to my house for tea. I'd love to hear all about it."

With the sound of her voice, memories had come flooding back to me, by no means all of them pleasant. I remembered Mum and her in the lounge, laughing and joking about her pronunciation. But I also remembered Dad's savage beatings, my intervention to try to save Mum, and the dark horrors that followed.

I didn't say anything about the trouble and trauma her English lessons had led to in our household. I didn't mention Mum getting beaten up by Dad, or why Mum had stopped her from coming. I feared that it might upset her. And I certainly didn't want to say anything about how Dad had used her visits as an excuse to focus his violent and abusive ways on me.

Edith Smith wasn't responsible for what had happened. The only person who was responsible for Dad's violence and sick behavior was Dad.

Even as my life changed and improved, I continued to discover stains from my past creeping into the present.

❀ ❀ ❀

Before leaving for university, I decided to get baptized to celebrate and reaffirm my conversion. It was another step toward growing in my faith and celebrating my free choice as a free person in a free society.

In a bold move, I decided to invite my family.

I wanted them to see how important my newfound faith and identity were to me. I wanted them to witness the freedom I was experiencing after escaping from my cultural ghetto. At the service, I planned to talk about discovering who I was and what I could do: speaking in public, traveling to India to help others, studying hard and winning a place at university, and building meaningful friendships.

I hoped it might open my family's eyes. Beyond that, however, I wanted to show them I had forgiven them. I knew how important the concept of forgiveness was in my newfound faith, and it was something that I was determined to live by. Inviting them to my baptism was a way of saying to them that they were forgiven—apart from my father. I didn't believe I could ever forgive my father.

I knew I was being hopelessly naive by inviting my family. I knew it might be foolhardy or even dangerous, but I thought it was worth the risk. At this stage, I had never heard the word "apostasy." I didn't know that it says in the *Hadiths*—the collected traditions about what the prophet Mohammed said, did, permitted, and prohibited—that anyone who converts out of Islam and refuses to return should be killed. But even had I known this, I think I would still have invited my family. The joy of my current life seemed more relevant than some ancient texts that no one would take literally.

I rang up Billy. For a while we chatted about family, and then I brought up the baptism. "Billy, I want you to come. It's something that's very special to me. I'd really like you to be there, and Mum, and Raz, and everybody."

Billy just snorted. I plowed ahead and told him the date and the place. Then, after a second or so of silence, my brother Billy hung up on me.

It was like a door slammed in my face. I was upset, but not entirely surprised. *Well, there's my answer,* I thought. *They're not coming.* Billy was the most liberal of the lot of them, so if that was his reaction I had no hope with the others. I took a deep breath. There was nothing more I could do now.

A few days later I was studying alone in the house. It was mid-afternoon when suddenly I heard a wild commotion outside. I ran to the window. In the street below was a mob of close to forty Pakistani men armed with hammers, sticks, and knives. Dad stood at the front, his face a mask of hatred and fury. To my horror, even my more liberal Uncle Kramat was there, shouting and yelling wildly like the rest. I couldn't see any of my brothers, or any of the women from East Street, but I didn't stay at the window to study the crowd in detail.

I rushed into the rear of the house to hide. I knew the front door was locked, but with forty screaming men outside, it could easily be smashed down. I had a vision of the mob surging up the stairs, their weapons brandished before them, their eyes wild with hatred and blood lust.

Even from the back of the house, beneath a bed, I could hear the uproar.

"Filthy traitor!" Dad thundered. "Traitor! Traitor! Traitor! You betrayer of your family! *Betrayer of your faith!* Cursed traitor! We're going to rip your throat out! We'll burn you alive!"

There was a pounding and a hammering on the door. I crawled further under the bed, shaking with fear, and I prayed to God to protect me.

I heard the letter box rattle, and suddenly Dad was screaming through it: "Filthy, dirty traitor! *Traitor!* We're going to cut you up! Slice you! Burn you! Rip out your traitorous heart. Traitor—you'll rot in hell!"

If Dad broke down the door, I knew I would be beaten to death by the mob.

CHAPTER 21

The Mob

❋

I was living in a white, working-class area where my father had no contacts, but somehow he found me. For what seemed like an age, the terrifying pounding of hammers and sticks on the door set a beat for the screamed curses, insults, and death threats.

Then suddenly it was silent. I lay beneath the bed, barely daring to breathe. Were they inside the house sneaking up on me? Had they gone around back to scale the garden fence?

I finally plucked up courage to crawl out and creep forward to the front of the house. Still I heard nothing. The entire street seemed deserted. Just as quickly as the crazed mob had come, it had disappeared.

I could only imagine the locals must have come out onto the street and threatened to call the police. Maybe, for once in his life, Dad had been forced to admit he wasn't autonomous. This was a tough, white, working-class neighborhood whose residents wouldn't have taken kindly to their street being invaded by a screaming *"Paki"* mob.

Still, I was shaking uncontrollably. I knew I was lucky to be alive. I dialed Rachel's number.

"Rachel, it's Hannan," I whispered, in a trembling voice.

"Hannan! What's wrong? Are you okay?"

"No. Yes. I mean—something terrible's happened. I'm really, really scared. I need your help, Rachel—"

"What?" I could hear the fear in her voice. "What is it? What's happened? Tell me!"

I was worried that if I told her the threat I faced from Dad and the mob, Rachel wouldn't help me. I was worried she would be too scared to come. In my panic, I told her the minimum I could, to get her to come to my aid.

"Look, I can't talk over the phone. Can you come? I'm at the house. I need you, Rachel. I really do."

"Of course. I'm on my way. Don't worry."

I stuffed my few possessions into a bag. Five minutes later I heard a car pull up and a knock at the door. When I peeped outside, relief flooded through me. It was Rachel. I ran out and dove inside her car.

We made straight for Rachel's house, where I stayed for several days. I only told Rachel and her family that my family had threatened me and I needed to get away from the house.

Not for one moment had I thought Dad would react with such a public show of extreme aggression and violence. His beatings and abuse had always been done in secret. But now the violence was out in the open, and the community was right behind him.

Over and over I pictured the faces of my family, and relatives, and the men from my street, twisted into masks of hatred. Each one knew me, and each was threatening vengeance against me — and death — all because I dared imagine I was free to choose my own faith.

I went ahead with my baptism anyway. Because my family knew which church I was planning to attend, I had to change the venue. Rachel pressed me to call the police and report Dad, but I resisted. The reasons were the same as before. I wanted to get on with my life, and I didn't want the implosion of my family on my conscience the rest of my days.

Even so, my life changed radically. I went into hiding and ended all contact with my family.

※ ※ ※

A few weeks later Skip warned me that my family — and the entire street — was looking for me, and I needed to be very careful. A dark anger simmered in the community over "one of their own" leaving Islam. Everyone knew girls sometimes fled forced marriages, but leaving Islam — that was beyond the pale.

I was worried about Skip, but she stood up to my family and protected me every time. Whenever someone discovered where I was living, the buzz went around the community, and Skip would warn me to flee.

My family told Skip I had to renounce Christianity, and until I did, they would hunt me down without rest. Only when I returned to them, to Islam, and to the man they had chosen for me to marry, would the threat to my life end. By now I was aware that my crime — apostasy — was the absolute worst thing I could have done.

It was emotional overload. All I wanted to do was stay hidden and live my new life.

❋ ❋ ❋

During the year after my father led the mob to attack me, I was forced to move every three months or so. I stayed with friends, families of friends, or in temporary rooms rented here and there. I was always ready to move at a moment's notice if I was warned that my family had tracked me down. I lived out of one bag and never settled down.

I anglicized my name from Hannan to Hannah, though I didn't kid myself that I would be any harder to find. I was living from day to day, almost totally unable to plan for the future. I saw my dreams of university fading as the dangerous game of cat and mouse continued.

It was impossible to feel settled, to study, or to hold down work for long. I felt as if I had physically escaped from my father, yet I remained imprisoned in an emotional nightmare.

It was two years after the mob that I finally felt able to take theology and religious studies at Lancaster University. My conversion to Christianity hadn't diminished my fascination with other faiths and belief systems. I noticed that one of the options on the syllabus was

"Islamic Feminism." Needless to say, I was fascinated by what that might be!

I didn't know what I wanted to do after university. Perhaps I would become a teacher like Felicity, or a social worker like Barry—the two people I looked up to most. But I knew I wanted to help young women who were trapped like I was. More and more stories were appearing in the press about girls running away from forced marriages, and about so-called "honor killings" facilitated by networks of Muslim family members and friends.

Each Friday at the mosque on East Street, my father handed out a photocopied mug shot of me with his phone number printed on the bottom. All across town, a network of spies tried to keep tabs on me. When someone saw me on the street, my father would assume I was living in a specific area. With more sightings, he could narrow down exactly where my house might be.

I thought about moving away from the north of England to escape from my family and their spy network once and for all. But all of my friends were here. And it was at Lancaster I had secured a place to study for my dream degree. Lancaster was a large, multi-ethnic city, I reasoned. I could sink into its urban anonymity and forget all about my pursuers.

Surely I'd be safe there.

CHAPTER 22

The Certainties of Ignorance

✳

My first few days at university were ones of total freedom. Suddenly it didn't matter what I wore, what I looked like, what color my skin was, or what I believed. I was surrounded by people of every race, color, and creed imaginable.

One of the first things I decided to do was read the Qur'an in English. After years of being told what to believe by holy men like my father, I needed to see what the Qur'an said for myself. As a child I had memorized many verses in Arabic, yet I never understood more than a few words.

I bought an English translation and started reading it at home, in the evenings, after my lectures and homework were done. Sure enough, there *was* the wrath and anger that my father had vented on me, but there were also many more gentle, humane verses, including ones about giving money to the poor and looking after widows and orphans. The milk of human kindness was to be offered to whomever was in need, regardless of their color or creed.

As I read the Qur'an for the first time, I realized that many of the things Dad had told me were fictions, while other ideas had been twisted into a rigid creed of exclusion and control. I noted, for example, that the Qur'an didn't prescribe specific words or the actions to accompany prayer. The ritual of standing, kneeling, and bowing one's forehead on the ground facing toward Mecca didn't appear anywhere, nor did the injunction to pray five times a day at specific times.

According to my father, performing those five daily prayers was the very essence of Islam. Strict adherence to such prayer was a Muslim's surest path to Paradise, even though those details were drawn from the *Hadiths*, and not the Qur'an.

I read it from cover to cover, and then I read it again. I was deeply angered when I discovered nothing whatsoever about arranged marriages. Dad told me repeatedly that the Qur'an instructed every Muslim parent to arrange marriages for daughters. In truth, the Qur'an doesn't seem to support forced marriages, as it states specifically that widows cannot be given to new husbands against their will.[4]

I was astounded to learn the Prophet Mohammed married his first wife, Kadija, for love. She was a wealthy older woman who had been widowed. He was employed by her as a trader, and over time they fell in love. Kadija wasn't related to Mohammed. In fact, they came from different tribes. So where on earth did the idea come from that young Muslim women should be forced to marry their cousins?

Other things amazed me, too. At its most basic, the Qur'an is Allah's word as revealed to his prophet, Mohammed. But it was not the story of Mohammed's life. It was a book of many stories: of Jesus' (*Isa's*) birth, of how the Angel Gabriel came to Mary (*Maryam*) and told her how Jesus was going to be born as a prophet sent by Allah. The story of Isaac and Ishmael, and the story of Abraham's (*Ibrahim's*) wife and her slave. The tales about Moses (*Musa*), Jacob (*Yaqub*), Joseph (*Yusuf*), and Job (*Ayub*).

There was a chapter about how Muslim women should be treated. It said that *both* men and women should dress modestly, and women should be cherished and protected. It did say husbands were allowed to beat their wives for ill-conduct,[5] but there was nothing about women being veiled head to toe or covering their hair and faces.

I also discovered that the Qur'an described a wife in an undermining way in Surah 2:223, which said that a wife was *tilth* for her husband: plowed land, ready for cultivation.[6] The notes and commentary in the English version of the Qur'an I was using interpreted this as meaning: "You can have sexual relations with your wife in any manner, as long as it is in the vagina and not in the anus."

In other words, a wife's worth was her fertility. She was to be impregnated or "cultivated" so that she might reproduce. The verse was not meant to protect the wife, but to point out that her only value was for carrying the husband's child.

On my second reading I counted the number of times Jesus was mentioned. There were ninety-five, while Mohammed was mentioned only twenty-seven. How had my father been able to yell at me that I wasn't even allowed to mention Jesus' name in our house? The Qur'an spoke of Jesus as a healer who performed miracles, not as a pariah.[7]

The Qur'an was certainly *not* the Qur'an taught by my father. I spent hours and hours studying what it *was* about, and the *Hadiths* that accompany it. I paid particular attention to the issue of converting out of Islam —so-called apostasy. It did indeed say that a Muslim could kill a fellow Muslim who turned away from Islam and refused to return. But I doubted whether my father actually knew this, considering his other glaring misapprehensions. I knew that my father's desire to kill me —and the bloodlust he had whipped up within the community—was more about the community's traditions of honor and shame.

Prior to reading the Qur'an, I presumed that what my father taught was Islam. Now I knew the truth. Very little of his most dogmatic beliefs and blind prejudices were in the holy book of Islam. For him to equate his prejudices with Qur'anic law constituted a level of ignorance, arrogance, and hypocrisy that was breathtaking — and sacrilegious.

Of course, other *imams* in the sort of community I came from said much the same kinds of things. My father's generation never questioned elders or teachers. Religious learning was based around an oral tradition, where things were passed down and learned by rote. The potential for misrepresentations to be magnified time and time again was immense.

For the first time in my life, I had no need to trust my father's version of Islam. I believed what I had read for myself.

CHAPTER 23

Hunted

❊

During my final year at university, Skip warned me my family had discovered where I was studying. One morning shortly after Skip's call, I saw, out the window of the bus, my brother Raz waiting at the college gates.

I had seen Lancaster University and academia as my inviolable sanctuary. Now that illusion shattered. After two years of living a relatively normal life, I knew I had to move right away. How much did my family know about me already?

I would have to become a nomad again.

I pushed back past the other passengers and stayed on the bus. Raz gave no sign that he had spotted me, so I kept my head down as the bus pulled away and phoned a close friend at the next stop. Could I stay with her for a few days? I needed to finish my degree and wasn't prepared to let my family ruin that. I couldn't let them win.

I sneaked back into college using a rear entrance, and went directly to speak to my lecturer in philosophy, Dr. Law, a man I liked and trusted. Over the years we'd had many interesting discussions about faith, tribe, and identity. He knew I'd converted out of Islam and had no contact with my family. Dr. Law notified the administration not to give out my contact details to anyone. Security was told to be extra vigilant.

The next day I discovered a note in my box from Raz. They were getting closer to me.

> *This is a note from your brother, Raz.*
> *You must get in touch.*
> *We really need to speak to you.*
> *This is my number.*

How had they tracked me down? When I called Skip, everything became very clear. Jamila, one of the Muslim women on my course, had become a friend of sorts. We found some common ground talking about Bollywood movies, the charts, and whatever was on television. What Jamila never told me was that she lived on the same street where Raz ran a shop. Through Raz, Jamila had met my family, and told them I was in a course with her at Lancaster University.

I confronted Jamila on the campus.

"I hear you told my family where I'm living. Why did you do that?"

Jamila wouldn't meet my eyes. "Look, I just ran into your brother at his shop, that's all. He knows my uncle, and I knew they were looking for you, so I just thought I should tell them. What's so wrong ...?"

"Do you have any idea what you've done?" I cut in. "Have you any idea how dangerous this is for me?"

"What do you mean? It's got nothing to do with me."

"Nothing to do with you! Let me tell you—it does now! You've got yourself involved by telling them where I live."

I stalked off, my fury mixed with fear.

I never made contact with Raz, even though he appeared on campus quite a few times. I don't think my brother intended to hurt me, but I didn't want him to become an extension of my father's rage. My last contact with my family had been in the form of a lynch mob, and I had no desire for a repeat performance.

My naïve hopes of a family reunion withered and died. Instead, I regularly prayed for my family, hoping against hope that in time they would come to understand me—and themselves. I prayed Mum would be well and that my sisters would be happy. I prayed for reconciliation with my brothers.

From time to time, I even prayed for deliverance for my father.

❋ ❋ ❋

I used the end-of-term vacation to work for a Christian charity in Greece. I hit it off with one particular family who hailed from the up-market southern English town of Farnham. Talking to them made me consider escaping properly. The only way to truly break free was leaving the north of England completely. I had to move where I wouldn't always be stumbling into people connected to my past.

During my final term, I applied for several jobs in Farnham. The YMCA came through with an offer of accommodation and a living wage, and I jumped at the chance, packing my few possessions and heading for the sunny south of England.

Farnham was the first place I lived where there were almost no Pakistani Muslims. I could walk from one end of the high street to the other without seeing one Asian face. No one seemed to pay me much attention, either, and for the first time in my life I felt like I could disappear in the crowd.

The anonymity made me feel safe. I'd lived with the feeling of being hunted for six years. Suddenly, the fear and the uncertainty were no longer there.

My work with the YMCA was chiefly in schools, helping with religious studies lessons. I also helped any homeless people who came into the hostel, teaching them a little independence so they could move on with their lives. Most were running from something, so I felt their situations were not so different from my own.

But for me, the running was over. At times I caught myself panicking: *I've been here too long! I have to get on a train and move on or else they'll find me!* But then I would take a deep breath, and tell myself that I was safe. I knew I could put down roots at last. I enrolled in a teacher training course. I moved into a house with some friends from my new church. In one sense, I was living the life I'd always dreamed about.

But as my fear gradually subsided, it was replaced by an aching sense of loss. I missed my little sister, my brother Billy, and my mum. Throughout the day I thought about what they might be doing. Here, in Farnham, where there was no possibility of seeing anyone from my family, I was confronted by how alone I was.

When I stopped running physically, it became clear that I had to stop running psychologically. I could no longer hide from the sexual abuse I had suffered. The time had come to face it.

I knew I needed to walk into the darkness and banish it once and for all.

CHAPTER 24

Finding Me

✽

Coming to terms with the sexual abuse that poisoned the first sixteen years of my life was daunting. I still felt it was partly my fault. What had I ever done to stop my father? I hadn't run. I hadn't told anyone. I still carried the shame, and it poisoned every other relationship in my life. When friends told me they loved me, I couldn't stop myself from thinking: *But would you still say that if you knew all about me?*

That damage didn't simply go away when the abuse stopped. I continued to feel dirty and guilty. I had hidden it for so long, my shame was almost overpowering.

In Farnham I met a girl named Samantha, and we soon became best friends. Samantha was laid-back and bursting with energy at the same time. She was petite, with dark hair and smoky eyes. What was more, she had a huge heart. There seemed to be no limit to her ability to give.

We met at church, and in no time Samantha had enveloped me with love. Over time, she and her family adopted me as the Joneses had done. I moved into a rented house with Samantha and her brother, Chris. We lived together like a family, cooking our favorite dishes for each other and talking long into the night.

With my increasing feeling of security, I let my mental and emotional defenses down. I started having nightmares and flashbacks to the darkest hours of the abuse —things I had kept long buried. Samantha sat up with me throughout the long nights when I was too scared to fall asleep again. Gradually, I revealed to her the full horror of my past. Samantha held me close to her for hours on end, as if her strength might help take away the pain and hurt.

For the first time in my life, I trusted someone to know everything about me. Samantha's response, God be praised, was love.

❊ ❊ ❊

One day I went into the town center to shop, but instead found myself wandering, lost and confused, in an area I'd never seen before. Hours passed. Disoriented and scared, I called Samantha. As I described the buildings I could see, she worked out where I was.

"Sit tight!" she said. "I'm coming to get you!"

More than three hours of time were a total blank. I had no memory whatsoever. It terrified me, but I put it down to exhaustion. Over time, however, it started happening more often.

I went to see my doctor, who diagnosed me with

depression and prescribed medication. But I was reluctant to take the pills. If I was depressed, there was a reason, and taking pills might treat the symptoms, but not the cause.

Instead, I went to a private, faith-oriented counseling service. The counselors talked to me about my past, about the nightmares and insomnia, and about the blackouts wherein I was losing myself for hours. Slowly, I began to open up about the worst aspects of the abuse. Finally, I even discussed what happened to me in the cellar.

"Hannah, I'm starting to think you may be suffering from PTSD," my counselor remarked during a session.

We'd been talking for several months, and I had really grown to trust her.

She explained that anyone exposed to extreme trauma can suffer from post-traumatic stress disorder, or PTSD. Soldiers who have seen awful things often find themselves suffering from PTSD, as do policemen, firemen, and the victims of violent crime.

At church, my vicar had prior experience with PTSD sufferers — most of whom were British soldiers. He was a great support to me. Only by talking about the trauma can a PTSD sufferer be cured. I decided I wanted to understand what I had suffered and deal with it accordingly, so, over time, I put together my own treatment regimen.

I discovered a retreat center in the Cotswolds called Harn Hill, a place of total peace, set among green hills, with sheep and cows grazing in the fields. It is a faith-based healing center, where people talk through the trauma they have suffered, pray together, and meditate.

My first week at Harn Hill was magical. I began to spend time there whenever I could, seeking the peace and the space to deal with my past. By talking about what had happened openly, I found I could slowly release the hurt and the pain. Coupled with the counseling, I felt myself becoming well again. Eventually, I reached a stage in my journey I thought would remain over the horizon forever.

I was ready to forgive my father.

CHAPTER 25

Finding Love

❋

On Christmas Eve 2006, I was at St. Bride's Church, in Farnham. The church was a traditional Anglican building with stained glass windows and beautiful stone pillars. That night the candles in the windows gave a beautiful warm glow all around the room. The large Christmas tree was covered in beautiful decorations and the smell of mince pies hung in the air. There were rows of people excited to celebrate the birth of Jesus together.

It was midnight service, and I was one of those chosen to give a reading. I had already done my part and the service was almost over when a young man turned around and stared at me. For a moment I caught his eye, but looked away again just as quickly. What was he staring at?

He didn't seem able to stop. To me, it was unnerving and rude. When the service finished, he hurried off to speak to a mutual friend of ours.

"*Who* is that beautiful girl?" he demanded of Jenny.

"Which beautiful girl?" Jenny countered. "There are quite a few here tonight, or hadn't you noticed?"

"That one," he replied, Jenny's teasing going completely over his head. "The one who gave the reading. The one with the big brown eyes and gorgeous hair and ... "

"All right, all right," Jenny stopped him. "I know who you mean. It's Hannah. Come on, I'll introduce you."

Jenny introduced Tom, inventing some nonsense about how she thought Tom and I should meet because I was a convert from Islam and Tom was fascinated by Islam. Almost immediately Tom started going on about this and that, and an instant later he was asking for my phone number. Though I had adjusted to life as a single woman, I was not accustomed to being shown such naked interest from the first handshake.

I told Tom I wasn't going to give him my number. I thought he was a bit forward, demanding to have it so quickly. He was persistent despite the signals of disinterest I was sending him.

He *did* have gorgeous blue eyes, I had to admit. But still, whatever it was he felt that first night, I simply wasn't feeling it.

Tom wasn't put off by the lukewarm reception. Instead, he talked Jenny into handing over my number. The next day he called me up.

"Hi, it's Tom. Remember me? From the church ... "

"Yes ... kind of," I replied, cautiously. "How on earth did you get this number? I seem to remember refusing to give it to you."

"I'll tell you how I got your number if you let me come round to visit you later today, okay? Deal?"

I had to give him a ten out of ten for perseverance. Samantha and Chris would be in the house, so I didn't see how it could do any harm. And anyway, a small part of me was intrigued. Who was this guy?

"Fine. Okay. Come round for tea or something ... "

A few hours later Tom turned up, admitting that he had talked Jenny into giving him my number. He spent an hour sitting on our couch, babbling on about who knows what. He was a whirlwind of words and nervous energy, asking me question after question without giving me time to answer. He hardly seemed to notice that Samantha and Chris were there.

What an oddball, I thought, *I'll just have to hope he keeps out of my way.*

Jenny called later. "So? *So?* What d'you think of Tom then?"

I told her the truth, that I wasn't exactly a fan and I was already thinking of ways to avoid him the next time he turned up. Jenny cracked up laughing and did her best to convince me I'd misjudged him and completely overlooked his appeal. "Come on, don't be too harsh. Poor Tom. He's not that bad. He's got amazing eyes ..."

Tom's next approach was via text messaging:

> *Please come and see me in Southampton.*
> *The community. We need it.*
> *There's lots of Muslims here. Tom.*

What on earth was that all that about? I texted back:

OK. I'll come when I find the time.

As in: Never.

I was swamped with work, and it was hard to find time to buy food, let alone hang out with Tom. I was running a series of workshops about Islam and cross-cultural issues for a charity called Crossways that helps people from different backgrounds better understand Islam—both the belief system and the culture that often goes with it. I focused on helping Muslim girls communicate with their parents about issues like arranged marriages. The aim was to begin dialogue before shame and honor did their dirty work.

At one of those workshops, Tom wandered in an hour early and told me how fascinated he was by the issues I was raising. He had come to listen and to learn, and could he help me set up? He was all fingers and thumbs, and when my talk ended he didn't want to leave.

"Tom, you really do have to go," I told him, eventually. "I have to pay for this hall by the hour. You've got a minute to make yourself scarce *or you're paying*!"

I even offered him a lift to the train station, just to get him out of the way. However, my boss at Crossways knew exactly what was going on, telling me Tom fancied me.

"That's impossible," I'd say. "He's just fascinated by Islam and stuff. Anyway, I hope not. I always end up with the odd ones ..."

At the next workshop Tom was there again. I was giving a talk on clothing and was wearing a *shalwar kamiz*.

Tom gazed at me and smiled shyly. "You look ... serene," he remarked dreamily. "Just so serene."

I wasn't quite sure what he meant by that, but I smiled politely. At least the *shalwar kamiz* wasn't canary yellow!

There was a piano at the back of the hall, and rather than get in my way afterward, Tom simply sat down and opened the keys. As his hands flashed over black and white, I stared at the back of his blond head. He played like a blazing angel. The music flowing from him captivated me.

As the final note hung in the air, the spell faded, but for a moment I had seen another side of Tom — a side that I could maybe, possibly ... like. Unbidden, a thought popped into my mind: *Maybe I need to give this guy a chance.* When Tom was playing — and not babbling — I had the time to notice that he was actually a fine-looking young man.

Perhaps sensing the change in me that his piano playing had wrought, Tom invited me to have a day out with him in Southampton. This time, I accepted, and we had a wonderful time together. Once Tom relaxed a little and got over being tongue-tied, he was great company.

"Why not come and visit my church?" Tom asked me, shyly. "Come and meet my friends. I'm sure they'd love to hear all about your life."

I readily agreed. Not out of any obligation, but because I truly wanted to see him again.

"And, um, would you like to have dinner tonight?" Tom added.

Once again, I agreed readily.

On the way to the restaurant, Tom became his babbling self again. When we sat down to eat, I found out why. He had been trying to pluck up courage to tell me how he felt about me. He looked so nervous I started to think he was going to cop out. The food was so salty neither of us could eat it, and his face was getting more and more red. He rambled on and on about his best friend and what a great person he was. I started to wonder why he was talking about his friend when we're here to talk about us. *Does he want me to go out with his friend?* I thought. And then ...

"Hannah, I think you're hot," he blurted out. "You're a real babe! I really want to go out with you," he managed clumsily.

I smiled and almost laughed. "All right ... Well, let's take it slowly and give it a try."

That was May. By summer Tom and I were inseparable. We fell more and more in love. I looked forward to weekends when I would see him.

I was forever asking Tom about life, belief, and how he dealt with pain and painful situations. There was a struggle within me, as I suspect there is in every one of us, over how to deal with pain and hurt. On the one hand, you could shrivel into bitterness and recrimination. On the other, you could rise above all that, and take the risk once more to engage with the beauty and unpredictable, intoxicating riot of life.

You could choose to risk life throwing whatever it might at you, and acknowledge that pain and hurt are possible, but knowing that with these come love and the joy and the richness of human experience. I was determined to do the latter, and especially so in my relationship with Tom.

At that time, I had "The Invitation" by Oriah Mountain Dreamer pinned to the wall of my room. I felt it was a remarkably poetic statement — so true to my own life — and it summed up much of my own philosophy on human existence:

> *It doesn't interest me what you do for a living.*
> *I want to know what you ache for,*
> *And if you dare to dream of meeting your heart's*
> *   longing.*
>
> *It doesn't interest me how old you are.*
> *I want to know if you will risk looking like a fool*
> *For love*
> *For your dreams*
> *For the adventure of being alive.*
>
> *It doesn't interest me what planets are squaring*
> *   your moon.*
> *I want to know if you have touched the centre*
> *   of your own sorrow,*

If you have been opened by life's betrayals,
Or become shriveled and closed
From fear of further pain.

The last verse really, really touched me and spoke of how I felt.

I want to know if you can be alone
With yourself
And if you truly like the company you keep
In the empty moments.

After the first sixteen years of my dark and abusive life, I reckoned I was just starting to reach the stage where I could be alone with myself and like who I was "in the empty moments."

I hoped Tom did too.

One day I found Tom reading "The Invitation" intently. Once he was done he turned to me and said, "Wow! You're deep."

"I hope so," I said, meeting his eyes. "I've lived too much to be shallow."

It wasn't long after that I began to tell Tom some of what had happened to me as a child. Of course, I feared that Tom might run, but I couldn't face the possibility of our relationship being based on a lie. When Tom told me he loved me, I needed it to be the real me he was loving.

Tom had to know. If he truly loved me, he wouldn't turn away. He would face me, betrayed and bruised as I was. And if he did that, Tom would be the one for me.

❋ ❋ ❋

Christmas Eve, 2007, and it was just before the midnight service at St. Bride's church once again. Tom asked me to meet him outside the church at 7:30 p.m., but he wouldn't tell me anything else. As I got dressed up ready to celebrate another beautiful Christmas, butterflies were soaring in my stomach and I wondered what he was planning.

I arrived at the church on time, but Tom was late and I was getting cold. Suddenly he appeared behind me and led me by the hand into the church. As we walked through to the back, he had laid roses up along the spiral staircase. When we entered the youth room on the second level, I noticed he had decked it out with all the things I loved—roses, lavender, and a purple tablecloth, which covered a table laid out for a candlelit dinner for two. I could smell curry, my favorite dish, and he wanted to wash my feet. When we both looked down and realized I had tights on, we just laughed.

Tom couldn't wait any longer. He got down on one knee and asked me if I would marry him, presenting a ring to me as he said those words I thought once I'd never hear.

I barely hesitated before saying: "Yes! I will!"

Later in the midnight service, the vicar announced the happy news of our engagement, and there was a spontaneous round of applause and cheering. Most of the people knew me, as it had been my church for eight years. As they cheered us on, I smiled deeply, inside myself.

I had finally said yes to "Oddball" Tom. It's funny — the way he tells our story, he's the knight in shining armor.

Maybe a person can be both.

CHAPTER 26

Lavender Dreams

✳

Being in love gave me the strength to try contacting my family again. None of them had apologized or shown regret for what they had done to me. It was all about what I had done to them: dishonoring my father, besmirching the family name, and so on. Even so, they were my family, and I would never get another one.

I managed to connect with my youngest sister, Aliya. She and I had always got on well, and she'd never been the perfect Muslim daughter like Sabina. We made a little stilted small talk over the phone before I got down to saying what I wanted to say.

"I could come to visit you," I suggested. "I could bring my flat mate, Samantha. She's really nice. You'd like her."

Aliya sounded horrified. "How could you do that to Mum and Dad? After all that you've done, you'd try to bring a dirty *gori* infidel into this house?"

"I'm also a dirty infidel," I countered. "So where does that leave us?"

"Yes, I suppose you are ... you're unclean, like the rest of them. In fact, I doubt if I'd even want to be in the same room as you."

The conversation didn't last much longer. I hung up and stood in shock at how my little sister had changed. The blind prejudice and hatred of my father had seeped into her veins too.

Soon after I received a text message from Raz:

> *Come back to Islam right now.*
> *Unless you do, you are an apostate.*
> *I will not be responsible for my actions.*

I could hardly believe my gentle brother Raz, who had escorted me to school to receive my English prize all those years ago, had said such a thing. Dad had succeeded in remaking even Raz in his own image.

There was no way back to my family, and I was grief-stricken. It was like losing them all over again. I had always nurtured a flame of hope inside me that we might, someday, be reconciled. That flame was now extinguished.

I had committed the ultimate act of betrayal toward them — apostasy — yet the better person I had become owed nearly everything to that decision. My family refused to climb out of the dark cellar of their prejudice to see the lovely young woman their daughter had become, and I would never again leave my place in the light.

❋ ❋ ❋

My wedding was a lavender dream.

Tom and I met at St. Bride's Church, got engaged at St. Bride's Church, and would marry there, too, just at the end of the light and airy center aisle. The church, the invitations, the flowers, and even the napkins and tablecloths at our reception were decorated with lavender butterflies, like something from a dream. Yards of white satin enveloped me that morning, shoulders bare, with a single diamond gracing my nose. I felt like a princess, with the tiara on my head to prove it.

Tom, his best man, and the ushers wore matching top hats and tails, with single white roses in their button-holes. He looked so perfect in his black jacket, charcoal gray trousers, crisp white shirt, and lavender cravat. I realized, gazing at him, what a seriously handsome man I had netted in Tom!

Rachel and Samantha were my bridesmaids, and they each wore a dress in the same sublime hue of lavender.

Felicity and James traveled down from Bermford to help give me away.

When I arrived at the door of the church with Saman-tha's dad, Rachel and Samantha met me. As the music for my entrance started, I looked across the gathered wit-nesses and grinned from ear to ear. Samantha's father led me down the aisle, while Tom waited for me at the altar. I looked up the long, white path of flower petals and silk to the face of the man I loved more than any other.

The church was packed with friends and relatives. They'd volunteered to decorate the church, cook the food, take the photos and video, and do just about anything else they could think of to keep the costs down.

I hadn't changed my mind. There were no last thoughts. I gazed into Tom's eyes and said, "I do." And then Tom was allowed to kiss the bride. A huge cheer went up from the hall as Tom wrapped me in an enthusiastic embrace, and a kiss that just seemed to go on and on and on.

Tom always does seem to have his own special way of doing things.

At the reception, Jenny — the person most responsible for getting Tom and me together — sang "Summertime" for us. As we stood atop the stairs and welcomed our friends and relatives, Jenny's husky, chocolate-spiced voice sent shivers up my spine:

> *One of these mornings*
> *You're going to rise up singing*
> *Then you'll spread your wings*
> *And you'll take to the sky*

It was the summertime of my life. The Lavender Fields were real. Hand in hand with my lover, I stepped into their prodigal grace.

CHAPTER 27

Justice for Them

For every girl born a British Muslim who, like me, manages to escape, there are many more who do not. Many remain trapped in forced marriages and abusive relationships, living a life little better than slavery. I meet such women through the charities I work with, and I can tell you painfully little progress has been made.

I met one Bangladeshi family in which every member had converted from Islam to Christianity: the mum, the dad, four girls, and one ten-year-old boy. Their community exerted enormous pressure on them to return to Islam. Eventually, half the family converted back, and the little boy and the youngest daughter stayed with the parents. But the oldest three girls—twenty-one, eighteen, and sixteen years old—were determined to carry on being Christians.

These three girls were in grave danger, and their story isn't unique. There is a crying need for shelters where people in such situations can find refuge. The life-and-death situations I faced in my teens are no way for children of any religion to have to grow up.

The dangers faced by women who leave Islam or flee from forced marriages are increasing. A teenage Muslim girl was forced to drink bleach by her uncle and brother before being stabbed to death for refusing an arranged marriage.

Her mother watched it all happen.

Few are willing to talk about this in public. The media doesn't have access to such stories. There is little or no debate at the political level. Most organizations working in this field are forced to remain silent in order to retain access to these helpless women.

If this conspiracy of silence continues unchallenged, nothing will change. Where is the outcry? Where are the defenders of human rights, women's rights, and religious rights, crying out for justice? Instead, time after time I hear of girls suffering the same fate as almost befell me. I hear of girls taking their own lives.

What I hear about is only the tip of the iceberg. For each rare case that makes it into the courts or the press, many more are covered up and silenced. Imagine how easy it would have been for my father to silently ship me off to Pakistan. Who would have spoken up on my behalf? Imagine how simple it would have been to deal with my refusal to leave, by murder if necessary. Imagine how the community would have closed ranks and protected him, throwing a blanket of silence over the disappearance of his daughter.

I escaped from an Asian Muslim ghetto. Not everything about the culture, the belief system, and the community that I left is evil. There is much of great value: community cohesion, respect for elders, a strong sense of identity, values informing modesty and good behavior. There are aspects of the community and family I left that I still miss.

Yet there is much that needs to be broken down, built up again, and mended.

CHAPTER 28

Silence Broken

❀

One day I had a phone call from one of the charities that I worked with. They explained that there was a television documentary being made about arranged marriages, by Channel Four, one of Britain's foremost broadcasters. Would I be willing to be interviewed?

The producer made it clear I could pull out at any moment if I didn't feel safe and secure. She had drawn up a contract guaranteeing to protect my identity and agreeing not to show my face on screen, or anything else that might identify me.

It took a whole day to shoot the interview. I was only shown from behind, the camera concentrating on my feet or my hands — parts of me that revealed nothing of my identity.

The interviewer asked me why I ran away from home. I spoke about fleeing a forced marriage, about converting out of Islam and the "crime" of apostasy. I spoke about going on the run and being forced into hiding. I talked about the mob and the death threats.

"Are there other girls in this situation?" the interviewer asked.

"Yes, obviously," I replied. "A lot of young Muslim women are suffering as I did."

"What can be done to help them?"

"There's a real need to understand the challenges posed by Islamic culture," I said. "We need to provide escape routes for girls like me, because they are horribly trapped where they are right now. And we need to start talking about it. We need to open a debate. We need to get it into the open. Silence doesn't help. It makes it worse, in fact."

The program broadcast a few weeks after the filming. I watched it at home with Samantha and Chris. Both of them were pleased for me, and proud I'd had the guts to speak out.

After that broadcast, more requests came for interviews. There was a call from a journalist with a flagship current affairs television program, among others. To journalist after journalist I told the story of fleeing a forced marriage, my conversion out of Islam, and being hunted by my family for so many years. I spoke about the concept of apostasy and how it often amounted to a death-sentence for the apostate.

Time after time, my interviewers were visibly shocked. How, they asked me, could such things be happening on the streets of Britain in the twenty-first century?

How indeed.

Once at the BBC radio studio, on the set of a well-known program, I was interviewed by a woman in her fifties. Near the end of our time, she leaned forward and asked, "So what do you hope to achieve by speaking out? Surely, you'll just cause more trouble?"

I'd rarely heard a more a stupid question. Would keeping quiet help the young girls and women trapped in situations like the one from which I had escaped? The question was part of a larger misapprehension that plagues Western civilization — that if we ignore a problem and don't cause any "trouble" it might all go away.

This I know: the problems that darkened the first sixteen years of my life will *never* go away on their own. Now, more than ever, we who cherish freedom of expression, freedom of political choice, and freedom of belief need to take a stand. We need to act.

Keep quiet to avoid trouble? I was going to *cause* trouble!

The next day I sat down and began to write.

From my childhood — the images sketchy and opaque, a splash of color here and there among darkness — I remember one thing clearly. My street. East Street.

Epilogue

This is my story and I have told it as accurately as my memory allows. Sometimes, the way we remember events is different than the way others do, and I apologize if I have made any significant errors in my story's telling. In my eyes, my life is not about misery; it is about love. The philosopher Sophocles once said, "One word frees us of all the weight and pain of life: that word is *love*." That is what I believe.

I was a caged butterfly and have flown free from what some would call the ghettoized Muslim community, but what I would call the trap of uninformed Islam. I seized hold of my freedom: freedom to choose what I believe; freedom to speak out about my beliefs; freedom to live a life as I see fit, even when others don't agree. I am a free woman in a world where there are many women encaged.

I am not the only woman who has thus grasped her freedom. There are others who have chosen to leave Islam, and therefore have become *murtadd*, or apostates. This is a story dedicated to them, too. As Jesus said, "In me you may have peace. In this world you will have trouble. But take heart! I have overcome the world." You can take heart and be free too. You only have to take the first and most difficult step.

In much of my life I felt fear that held me back from living, but I believe we all can live a life without fear — at peace with ourselves and others. As I look at this world, again and again I see fear: the politically correct fear of offending Muslims, the fear of Islamist terrorism, the fear Muslims have that they will all be branded as terrorists. We need to overcome this corrosive, vicious cycle of fear that breeds more fear. And the starting point of doing so is breaking the silence.

As Ayaan Hirsi Ali writes in her book, *Infidel*: "People ask me if I have some kind of death wish, to keep saying the things I do. The answer is no: I would like to keep living. However, some things must be said, and there are times when silence becomes an accomplice to injustice."*

I, too, cannot be silent about what happened to me, and what is still happening to countless other young girls and women today. I am concerned for the future of the Muslim community in my own democratic country, as well as in democratic countries around the world. I am worried for Muslim women who, like me, want to choose to live a free life in Britain, across Europe, in the US, and elsewhere, but cannot because of the straightjacket of honor and shame controlling many of them, and the entrenched attitudes of some communities they inhabit.

---

*Ayaan Hirsi Ali, *Infidel* (New York: Free Press, 2008).

Belief is a uniquely personal thing. Freedom to believe as the individual sees fit — or not to believe, for that matter — is a defining feature of civilization. If we no longer have the willingness or strength to defend people's freedom of choice in religion, then we have lost the very foundations of our civilization. If we go there, intolerance and totalitarianism will follow.

Since writing this book, I have spoken out widely about my story and the wider issues it raises. In the UK, the US, and elsewhere I have talked to gatherings of 5,000-plus people at a time. It was at first a daunting prospect, but I do this because I cannot be silent about injustice. And I shall keep doing so because I love life, and I love my fellow humans who inhabit this world.

> *Peace I leave with you, my peace I give you ...*
> *Do not let your hearts be troubled and do not be*
> *afraid.*
>
> JOHN 14:27

Islam-Related Religious Terms

(see also the list of Punjabi, Urdu, and Arabic terms)

A–G

Ayub—	Job
Bismillah—	central text of Islam
Deobandi Sunni Muslim—specific sect	

H

Hadiths—	writings of Mohammed
Hajj—	holy pilgrimage to Mecca
Hajji—	one who has been on the Hajj
Hajjin—	female who has been on the Hajj
hafiz—	a man who has learned at a madrassa

I

Ibrahim—	Abraham
imam—	leader of the mosque and/or community
Irahma—	as in Allah the Merciful
Isa—	Arabic word for Jesus, the prophet

J–L

jellabiya—	Muslim robe
Kaaba—	box building in Mecca
kiswah—	drape on the Kaaba

M–N

madrassa—	religious school
Malik—	as in Allah the Mighty
Maryam—	Jesus' mother

murtadd—	apostates
Musa—	Moses

P

Paki—	a British Pakistani who is loyal to home, a racist term; (*Pakis*, plural)
Paradise—	heaven, distinctly Islamic here
pir—	holy man, Muslim

Q

Qur'anic school—	religious school, *madrassa*

R

Rahim—	as in Allah the Forgiving
Ramadan—	Muslim holiday

S

sharia—	as in sharia law, Islamic law
surah—	chapter (in the Qur'an)

T

tasbih—	prayer beads
taviz—	holy necklace (not prayer beads)
topi—	skull cap

U–X

Ummah—	the people of Islam
wudu—	washing before prayers

Y

Yaqub—	Jacob
Yusuf—	Joseph

Punjabi, Urdu, and Arabic Words

A

    Ayub—   Job

B

    Bismillah—   central text of Islam
    burka—   women's covering

C–F

    chappati—   a type of bread; (*chappatis*, plural)
    Deobandi Sunni Muslim—specific sect

G

    gora—   white male
    goray—   white people
    gori—   white female

H

    Hadiths—   writings of Mohammed
    hijab—   article of clothing
    Hajj—   holy pilgrimage to Mecca
    Hajji—   one who has been on the Hajj
    Hajjin—   female who has been on the Hajj
    halal—   allowed; similar to the Jewish
                   term *kosher*
    halvah—   food
    haram—   forbidden
    hafiz—   a man who has learned at a madrassa

I

    Ibrahim—   Abraham

    imam—   leader of the mosque and/or community

    Irahma—   as in Allah the Merciful

    Isa—   Arabic word for Jesus, the prophet

J

    jellabiya—   Muslim robe

K–L

    Kaaba—   box building in Mecca

    kiswah—   drape on the Kaaba

M–O

    madrassa—   religious school

    Malik—   as in Allah the Mighty

    Maryam—   Jesus' mother

    murtadd—   apostates

    Musa—   Moses

P

    paisa—   coin

    Paki—   a British Pakistani who is loyal to home, a racist term; (*Pakis*, plural)

    pakoras—   a kind of food

    Paradise—   heaven, distinctly Islamic here

    paratha—   a food item; (*parathas*, plural)

    pir—   holy man, Muslim

Q

    quawwali—   music

    Qur'anic school— religious school, *madrassa*

R

Rahim—	as in Allah the Forgiving
rail—	book stand
Ramadan—	Muslim holiday

S

sag—	lamb curry
shalwar kamiz—	clothing worn
sharia—	as in sharia law, Islamic law
surah—	chapter (in the Qur'an)

T

tasbih—	prayer beads
tava—	a kind of pan
taviz—	holy necklace (not prayer beads)
tika—	gold pendant for the forehead
tilth—	fertile soil
tonga—	horse and cart
topi—	skull cap

U–W

Ummah—	the people of Islam
wudu—	washing before prayers

Y

Yaqub—	Jacob
Yusuf—	Joseph

Z

zakat—	charity

Notes

All direct Qur'anic quotations and commentary in this book are taken from *Interpretations of the Meanings of the Noble Qur'an (With Commentary)*, translated by Dr. Mohammad Taqi-ud-Din Al-Hilali and Dr. Muhammad Muhsin Khan.

1. "Do not kill yourselves." Surah 4:29

2. The Qur'an does speak of being a "slave" of Allah (other translations use "bondsman" or "servant"). Surah 3:15–30

3. The Qur'an says quite clearly that menstruation is an "indisposition" (other translations use "illness"), and that menstruating women are "unclean." Surah 2:222

4. Widows could not be forced to remarry against their will. Surah 4:19

5. Husbands were allowed to "beat" their wives for "ill-conduct" (other translations use "rebellion"). Surah 4:34

6. Wife was "tilth" for her husband. Surah 2:223

7. The Qur'an speaks of Jesus as a healer. Surah 3:44–49

Acknowledgments

Special thanks to my literary agents in the UK and the US, for your faith and belief that mine was a story that should be told. Very special thanks to Josephine Tait, a religious freedom campaigner whose advice, friendship, and help have proven invaluable. Thanks to Tom, for being an amazing husband and partner for life. Thanks to Lizzy and Mike, and family, who've given me a safe place to grow and to heal. Thanks to Felicity and James, for providing me with a way out and a gateway into the future.